Achieving value for money in capital build projects

This book is the first to bring together academic and practitioner views of value for money (Vf). VfM has been used to assess whether or not an organisation has obtained the maximum benefit within the resources available to it. A concept used by the public sector to assess the benefits of major built environment projects, it has become a major tenet of public private partnerships, capital project infrastructure and civil engineering megaprojects.

This book presents and discusses the various debates surrounding the concept of value for money. It provides an international perspective on VfM by drawing on the existing and fast developing body of principles and practices for capital build projects. Readers will gain a level of understanding of the issues involved, the challenges, opportunities and the support mechanisms and protocols required for implementation of VfM in capital building development.

Ultimately, the book presents a protocol that has been developed to track and monitor the VfM of a capital project from day 1, an Equilibrium Testing Mechanism (ETM) developed by the authors. This testing mechanism allows each of the parties to a project to monitor its VfM position at any given stage of a project from the beginning to the end of the build stage and beyond as necessary.

This book is both a useful reference for researchers and a practical guide for the construction and engineering industry.

Angela Vodden is a practising solicitor within her own firm but predominantly represents public sector clients, specialising in the strategic procurement and legal negotiations of high value public sector infrastructure and development projects.

Champika Liyanage is Associate Professor in Facilities Management in the School of Engineering, University of Central Lancashire, UK.

Akintola Akintoye is a Chartered Surveyor and a Chartered Builder. He is Professor of Construction Economics and Management and Dean of School of Built Environment and Engineering in the Leeds Beckett University, UK.

Spon Research

publishes a stream of advanced books for built environment researchers and professionals from one of the world's leading publishers. The ISSN for the Spon Research programme is ISSN 1940-7653 and the ISSN for the Spon Research E-book programme is ISSN 1940-8005

Published:

Soil Consolidation Analysis
978-0-415-67502-4
J.H. Yin, G. Zhu

OHS Electronic Management Systems for Construction
978-0-415-55371-1
I. Kamardeen

FRP-Strengthened Metallic Structures
978-0-415-46821-3
X. L. Zhao

Valuing People in Construction
978-1-138-20821-6
F. Emuze and J. Smallwood

**Preventing Workplace Incidents in Construction:
Data Mining and Analytics Applications**
978-1-138-08745-3
Imriyas Kamardeen

Construction Health and Safety in Developing Countries
978-1-138-31707-9
Patrick Manu, Fidelis Emuze, Tarcisio Saurin and Bonaventura H. W. Hadikusumo

Achieving Value for Money in Capital Build Projects
978-0-8153-6119-0
Angela Vodden, Champika Liyanage & Akintola Akintoye

Risk Management in Engineering and Construction: Tools and Techniques
978-0-415-48017-8
Stephen Ogunlana & Prasanta Dey

Achieving value for money in capital build projects

Angela Vodden, Champika Liyanage
and Akintola Akintoye

LONDON AND NEW YORK

First published 2019
by Routledge
4 Park Square, Milton Park, Abingdon, Oxon OX14 4RN
605 Third Avenue, New York, NY 10017

First issued in paperback 2023

Routledge is an imprint of the Taylor & Francis Group, an informa business

© 2020 Angela Vodden, Champika Liyanage and Akintola Akintoye

The right of Angela Vodden, Champika Liyanage and Akintola Akintoye
to be identified as authors of this work has been asserted by them in
accordance with sections 77 and 78 of the Copyright, Designs and Patents
Act 1988.

All rights reserved. No part of this book may be reprinted or reproduced
or utilised in any form or by any electronic, mechanical, or other means,
now known or hereafter invented, including photocopying and recording,
or in any information storage or retrieval system, without permission in
writing from the publishers.

Trademark notice: Product or corporate names may be trademarks or
registered trademarks, and are used only for identification and explanation
without intent to infringe.

British Library Cataloguing in Publication Data
A catalogue record for this book is available from the British Library

Library of Congress Cataloging-in-Publication Data
A catalog record has been requested for this book

ISBN: 978-1-03-257022-8 (pbk)
ISBN: 978-0-8153-6119-0 (hbk)
ISBN: 978-1-351-11694-7 (ebk)

DOI: 10.1201/9781351116947

Typeset in Goudy
by Taylor & Francis Books

Publisher's Note
The publisher has gone to great lengths to ensure the quality of this reprint but
points out that some imperfections in the original copies may be apparent.

Contents

List of illustrations	vi
Preface	vii

1 The historic development of value for money within the UK, China, Australia, South Africa and India   1

2 Tracking VfM: concept, definition, benchmark, tracking and testing   43

3 Stakeholder roles, responsibilities, expectations, aims, incentives and drivers   59

4 Identification of the value for money stages   77

5 The need for the VfM tracking mechanism   97

6 Value for money protocol, bid document and contract drafting: Final word   119

Index   125

Illustrations

Figures

2.1	A timeline of VfM tests	45
5.1	Senior debt funder	112
5.2	Senior debt funder	113
5.3	Equity funder	113
5.4	Construction contractor	114
5.5	FM contractor	115
5.6	The beneficiary group	115
5.7	Local government	116
5.8	Central government	117
5.9	Comparison of all stakeholder groups	117
6.1	Central government	123

Tables

3.1	Key drivers or incentives of each stakeholder group involvement	63
4.1	Identification of stakeholder group VfM value and fluctuations at each key stage	91
5.1	Identification of stakeholder VfM tracking values	100

Preface

We are delighted to introduce this unique text, which debates not only how and why the concept of value for money (VfM) became so important within a public sector arena, but also how its interpretation has different meanings for different people, industries and societies. Indeed, it is seen throughout the decades that the meaning of VfM develops as time, economies and societies advance, not just in the UK, but also within a global arena.

It is widely understood that the achievement of VfM is of paramount importance within public sector procurements globally, but yet when we truly scrutinise the contractual structures and standard form documents on which public sector infrastructure projects are undertaken, this importance does not seem to be evident. Even more shockingly, there is no method or system imposed throughout the contract period that requires the achievement or not of VfM to be tracked or addressed. Given the importance of VfM, this should be a fundamental element of any contractual document. This text provides a solution to this lacuna.

This book has evolved from research, and consultancy works that have been undertaken by the authors in public–private partnerships, joint venture developments and infrastructure procurements, through a variety of contractual solutions over a period of 20 years. However, in some parts of the world public–private partnerships are a relatively new way of procuring infrastructure and associated services, through which they have to share risk and deliver value for money solutions.

VfM has been used to assess whether or not an organisation has obtained the maximum benefit (in terms of economy, efficiency, effectiveness) from the goods and services it both acquires and provides, within the resources available to it. This is has particularly been used by the public sector in many parts of the world to access the benefits driveable from major built environment projects including civil engineering and building projects, In particular, this has become a major tenet of public–private partnerships capital project infrastructure and civil engineering megaprojects.

The contractual requirements for infrastructure development do not need to be a trigger that results in termination, if each party approaches the main goal, albeit for different reasons, with the same collaborative ethos. In essence, there is no reason why each party to a project cannot achieve a

viii *Preface*

"win–win" value for money solution as originally envisaged by Sir Michael Latham in his report "Constructing the Team".

In this book, we have illustrated an approach informed by our own research and experience of working with a diversity of parties involved in public–private partnership projects how a VfM agenda can be achieved. The book as a simple aim. It is written primarily to help and provide all stakeholders involved in an infrastructure procurement to understand the salient issues involved in achievement of VfM in projects, with an element of the historical needs for this. This book makes no attempt to cover all aspects of issues involved in infrastructure procurement. Our aim in this book is essentially to make the process of achieving VfM in project setup transparent, and easily achievable for the stakeholders from both the public and private sectors. It offers insight necessary to engage with VfM processes effectively and develop efficiency in doing so.

The book provides a full and coherent explanation of the concept of VfM and how that should be viewed among a number of participant groups within the built environment. This is unique as more often than not the concept of VfM is only considered important from a public sector viewpoint, yet every critic has a VfM viewpoint because of its subjectivity. The chapters in the book have been crafted in a stylistic way with many distinguished features, some of which are:

1   A discussion and critique of value for money from a diversity of interested parties and from many countries where value for money has been incorporated into the public sector policy for the procurement of goods and services (Chapter 1).

2   A review the current subjective nature VfM and lack certainty of definition and the fact there is no proactive requirement for any stakeholder engaged within a project to track VfM and a systematic failure to implement a mechanism to track, test and ultimately confirm whether VfM is being achieved (Chapter 2).

3   A critical discussion of the stakeholder's roles, responsibilities, expectations, aims, incentives, and drivers, in the way value for money is achieved and the impact on project objects and relevance to public sector procurement policies (Chapter 3).

4   A discussion of pinch points in VFM identification, implementation and achievements at various key stages of project development, with the overall aim of understanding where the VfM points might arise and how they can be tracked (Chapter 4).

5   Development of a VfM tracking mechanism within projects, on an ongoing basis, to identify whether projects were either achieving VfM or not, with the expectation that the reasons could be identified at each of the key stages for this outcome from the perspective of all stakeholders involved in the project development (Chapter 5).

6   Development of VfM protocol and impact on bid documentation and contract drafting with a reflection on how VfM tracking mechanism can

be implemented in a practical way and used within infrastructure project (Chapter 6).

The book provides an international perspective on VFM by drawing on the existing and fast developing body of principles and practices for capital build projects by bringing together academic and practitioner views of VFM. Within the overarching concept of capital build projects, the book draws on experience of how this is implemented in a public–private partnerships project environment. Hence the book is essential reading for academics, researchers, professionals and students in the built environment. It is also a useful tool to those practitioners in the public and private sector who are involved in how infrastructure projects and development projects are structured to inform the public sector value for money agenda.

Many thanks.
Angela Vodden
Champika Liyanage
Akintola Akintoye

1 The historic development of value for money within the UK, China, Australia, South Africa and India

Introduction

This chapter will look at when and why VfM evolved within the UK, China, Australia, South Africa and India as examples of different cultures at different stages of their own socioeconomic and political development, with all competing for a part within a global economy. By investigating the countries and their various stages of political, legal and socioeconomic growth through the ages, it becomes possible to highlight the stage or stages at which the achievement of VfM becomes important.

Value for money as a concept is subjective, its perception different at any given time or era for everyone everywhere irrespective of whether it is tested from a public or private sector viewpoint, which is why there are many facets to it and different incentives driving the need to achieve it. Only by understanding the political, legal and socioeconomic backgrounds of a range of developed and developing nations through the ages can the need for its implementation on a national and commercial level be understood and therefrom mechanisms advised or imposed as a means to test the actual achievement of VfM goals.

United Kingdom

Overview

VfM has, in one guise or another, been debated within the UK for centuries, even, it would appear, as far back as 1266, when Henry III set about fixing prices for bread and ale to correspond with corn prices. In 1349 King Edward III decreed that foodstuffs should be sold at reasonable prices.[1] Moving further along this VfM journey, it can be seen that, by 1857, as the powers of the government are extending and public spending is increasing, there is an acknowledgement that a mechanism by which to scrutinise public accounts is needed. the Public Accounts Committee in 1857 being the first mechanism introduced by parliament to undertake that role.[2] It is with this background in mind that it is interesting to witness through the ages how VfM, its interpretation and the need to achieve it has grown.

2 The historic development of VfM

Politics, society and economy: the early years

Prior to 1880, the social and welfare needs of the UK population had been catered for either by the farmers within the rural communities who housed their farmhands or the landed gentry who housed their employees within their estates and homes.[3] Tradesmen, industry workers, white- and blue-collar workers and the professions, where they could afford it, lived in private accommodation, boarding houses or other rented accommodation. The only social housing at that time was the workhouse; any other assistance that was available was voluntarily organised and piecemeal with minimum state intervention.[4]

As the 19th-Century industrial society advanced, the UK saw a significant shift in the workforce as the population migrated into towns and cities from the rural farming areas. As the workers moved into the cities to take up the opportunities in the new industries, the increase in demand for urban living space became evident. A housing shortage inevitably gave rise to the creation of slums, the infrastructure was inadequate and not able to cope with the increased demand, therefore poor sanitation resulted, which accounted for increased outbreaks of contagious diseases. The need to urgently address this change in demographic saw the introduction of reactive local government acts. This began the increase in the level of state intervention into people's lives within the UK.[5]

Central and local government administrations began to grow in conjunction with other large scale bureaucratic organisations and state powers were given to local administrations in relation to education, housing, public health, work and child welfare. These interventions and the cost of administering them grew rapidly and, by 1899, local councils' powers were extended to provide, manage and maintain education, transport (including highways), housing, public health, gas, water, lighting, food inspections, libraries and parks, among other social functions, and "as a more complex society grew, it was believed that there was a need for the administration of public spending to be more centrally controlled", this era being hailed as the "beginning of the golden age of local government".[6] It appears that from here on, the bureaucratic industry and the government machine began to grow and became increasingly complicated. In order to deal with this growth of administrative function wider scale legislative provisions were required and therefrom a self-perpetuating government industry arose.

It was recognised in early 1857, as the demands on the public purse were increasing to accommodate the needs of society, that "inquiry was needed into the receipt, issue and audit of public monies in the Exchequer, the Pay Office and the Audit Department".[7] It was not until 1862 that the Chancellor of the Exchequer, William Gladstone, established the Public Accounts Committee, expressing "that there shall be a standing Committee to examine the Accounts showing the appropriation of sums granted by Parliament to meet Public Expenditure."[8] This committee was borne from the need to strengthen parliamentary scrutiny over public finances as a mechanism to combat fraud and corruption as spending on equipment for the war effort was brought into question. In order to give impetus to this committee the Exchequer and Audit Act was passed, which was held by the Public Accounts Committee as a significant mark in the development of parliamentary control.

It is recorded that in 1887, the Public Account's Committee (PAC) stated that its remit was such that "if in the course of its Audit, the Comptroller and Auditor General becomes aware of facts which appear to him to indicate an improper expenditure or the waste of public money, it his is duty to call it to the attention of Parliament."[9] It was not, however, until 1904, when a full inquiry took place into the massive mismanagement of the South African war that questions were raised into the discrepancies of prices of purchasing horses, by the war office and from there on the PAC placed a new emphasis on "the importance of looking beyond the formality of the expenditure, but also, to its wisdom, faithfulness and economy". This perhaps can be held to be the first definition to be given to VfM, albeit unbeknown to the speaker of those words.[10]

It was also in the early 1900's that the UK was just starting to see the introduction of a properly functioning system of devolved administration and local government control of the towns and cities. This extension of public sector intervention in people's lives meant that there was an increase in the level of public spending, which in 1900, in the UK, equated to 12% of GDP.[11] This increased to 15% just prior to WWI to address growing demand, as the need for further state intervention became significantly apparent to address rising unemployment and socioeconomic unrest.[12]

Politics, society and economy: WWI (1914–1918) and its aftermath

In order for the UK to respond to the declaration of war and to ensure that the military forces had the equipment that they needed quickly the Public Accounts Committee relaxed its financial controls, recognising that there was a need to act urgently. The recommendation given was simply to "ensure they curbed excessive profits to their suppliers".[13] Whether it was as a result of the lack of scrutiny or simply the state of the nation is a moot point, but the biggest leap in public spending was just after WWI, when it almost doubled to 27%.[14] This was explained as being largely due to returning soldiers requiring increased healthcare, a rise in the unemployed needing welfare as women had taken up many of the jobs left behind by the men. Women's emancipation and job shortages being factors to be considered as an impact on the economy and just as importantly was the need to advance infrastructure to allow the country to develop economically to compete within the world markets.

The UK suffered economically because of the cost of the war, not simply in fiscal terms but in terms of lives lost, damage to infrastructure and an inevitable stagnation of entrepreneurialism outside the development of railway links across the British Empire.[15] The result was a lack of significant investment in the new industrial mass production technology in the UK

4 The historic development of VfM

both during the war because of the war effort and post-war as the country tried to rebuild itself. This meant that the UK had to import many industrial materials that, historically, it would have been able to obtain from its own industries. The imports the UK needed to make included the new fashionable goods that had been developed during the war period such as washing machines and refrigerators from its USA competitor.[16]

Alarmingly, the UK needed to import coal, its own reserves having been significantly depleted as a direct consequence of the war.[17] At this point (1918 onwards), more coal was being imported than was being mined nationally. The mining communities were feeling the strain: not only were the miners being exploited by the private enterprises that owned the companies, but they were being asked to work longer hours at reduced pay by the government. The mining industry was predominantly privately owned and control of production and output was undertaken by a coal controller, who dictated where the coal was mined from and how and where it was distributed, thus corruption was common. The cost of production of coal had escalated and disputes between the miners and the mine owners were a predominant feature, as a seven-hour day had been imposed by legislative provision within the mines, but the final straw came when the threat of a 49% wage cut was made.[18] The miners were fighting for better conditions, better wages and the nationalisation of the industry, rather than the private ownership position that they currently experienced across the different coalfield districts.[19]

Trade unions became increasingly active: the Miners Federation, National Union of Railwaymen and the National Transport Workers' Federation collaborated to form the triple alliance, giving rise to unrest and, ultimately, all-out action in the form of industrial strikes by each of the represented workforces.[20] In dealing with the pressure of the strikes, the UK economy fluctuated significantly presenting an uncertain market.

As the 1920s progressed, the UK still found it difficult to advance competitively having failed to meet both global and national changing demands for development in technology and industrialised processes. It was still the case that the commodities within which the UK usually traded such as cotton, steel, coal and iron were now globally oversupplied. Opportunities for the UK to export its manufactured and industrial goods became increasingly costly and difficult because of the protectionist import tariffs imposed by other countries, such as Germany and the USA, thus making it even more expensive for the UK to export those goods that it could. These actions meant that, in the UK, unemployment continued on a downward spiral as economic uncertainty continued.[21]

By 1925, Winston Churchill, UK Prime Minister at the time, determined that it was appropriate for the UK to return to the gold standard (being the measurement and value of the UK currency). While the UK had its currency measured against the gold standard, historically, there had been economic stability; however, far from achieving that outcome this decision resulted in a strong pound driving up interest rates harming businesses, combined with the underinvestment in the UK during the war period and other external factors such as the USA Wall Street Crash in October 1929, thereby increasing the economic strain on the UK, plummeting it into depression.[22]

As the problems grew, there was a shift in economic approach within the UK, from the laissez-faire principles of old to increasing state intervention within industry and nationalisation. The UK economy then, as it is now, was based on free trade but was focused on industrial and manufacturing opportunities predominantly in the north of the country, while the south prospered from trade, journalism and the finance industry.[23]

While economic division has always had an impact on the social classes, the class divide was becoming more apparent. The upper middle classes consisting of aristocracy, merchant traders, industrialists and financiers, were able to enjoy the fashionable goods, cars, telephones and the benefit of reduced working hours. Indeed, this was the era in which "holidays" became a popular pursuit, as reduced working hours paved the way for more leisure time. Yet, the ordinary working-class citizens experienced very little of this benefit.[24]

Unemployment had risen to just over 2 million people out of 45million of the total country's population and the poverty gap between the lower and working classes set against the middle and upper classes was significant at almost 20% (Joseph Rowntree Foundation). Welfare reform had not yet been implemented fully and welfare benefits at that time were not automatically available, thus the unemployed received little assistance; welfare was both insurance based and means tested and was still administered in the main by the parish councils under the Poor Laws.

As the UK worked through the 1930s, it witnessed the ongoing developments brought about by the continued industrial revolution, the impact of which caused furthering of the unemployment levels among farmers and the working classes who traditionally used manual methods of working. The new machinery and production line processes that were taking over were reducing the need for man power. The economy was also in flux as the true impact of being aligned to the gold standard was taking effect. The decision was taken to come off the gold standard in 1931, which made British goods cheaper again, however, protectionist measures of other countries, which remained in place during this period, were still hindering the UK's exports at a time when the UK economy needed to ensure that the exportation of its industrial and manufactured products continued. Thus, the rise in public spending steadily increased throughout the 1930s, not just to match public demand for the departmental services, but also to match the growing cost of operating such an administrative machine.[25] The Public Accounts Committee began once more to try and regain its control, criticising departments for failing to account and comply with required standards, but further stating "that it was imperative to secure the economy in every department of public (as well as private) life, if national bankruptcy was to be avoided",[26] a stark reality check of how precariously balanced the UK economy was at that time, as the focus of its work at this juncture was on the extravagance of wasted money, how departments were operating organisationally and staff deployment. Thus it would appear

6 *The historic development of VfM*

that the VfM focus is centred on not wasting money and inefficiencies within departments in times of economic flux.

By 1934 the PAC had successfully extended its authority to include within its focus how the awarding of contracts was being undertaken and how the pricing and fixing of profits was calculated and the UK government's position as a buyer within the country and oversees. However, this form and level of scrutiny was short lived. The onset of WWII meant that the rules once more had to be relaxed and non-compliances allowed. While these investigations by the Public Accounts Committee are referenced as being exercises in ensuring value for money, on the face of the documents, it would appear that the exercises relate more to ensuring that excessive profits were not given to the private sector and ensuring that the public funds were well spent to meet the socioeconomic challenges facing the UK. What is clear is that the early references to VfM do not relate to elements of quality or fitness for purpose. It was a matter of ensuring that public funds were well spent and that good financial management was prevalent within government departments.[27]

Politics, society and economy: WWII *(1939–1945)*

Outside the UK, Hitler had come to power and fascism was on the rise. Germany's expansionist policies and eventual invasion into Poland led Neville Chamberlain (Prime Minister at the time) to declare war on Germany (on 1 September 1939) and the UK's six-year involvement in WWII began.[28]

The wars in Europe took up the first half of the century, with rationing of food and clothes taking place in England. The USA contributed to the WWII effort again in the early years through its lend-lease approach by lending (in 1940s' terms):

British Empire: $31.4 billion
Soviet Union: $11.3 billion
France: $3.2 billion
China $1.6 billion

From a social perspective, however, the people of the UK during this period came together, bridging some of the historic class divides to pull the country together in pursuit of a common goal. This impetus was then used as the political tool and leverage by the Labour Party to achieve its victory just after the war: introducing the Beveridge Report in 1948, which extended the welfare provisions from those implemented in 1909 and provided the blueprint for the National Health Service as the answers to the end of the poverty-stricken lifestyles that the British had seen prior to the War.[29] While the advancement of welfare and healthcare was a good result of the time, the demands of the populous were also increasing in relation to housing and, while public spending was increasing to accommodate the demands and to give effect to infrastructure projects, so, too, was the level of national debt.

The taxation system in the UK has always been the method of collecting the finance for government expenditure. In order to keep up with the levels of public spending, the types and levels of taxation have increased and become increasingly complicated over the years. In 1944, the pay as you earn (PAYE) system for collecting income tax was introduced to make tax collection more efficient. Indeed, the introduction of taxes has seen the loss of office in the UK for many parliamentary figures.[30]

Post-WWII towards the accession into the European Union (1945–1972)

During the post-war period, the Labour government continued with its nationalisation policy by establishing the National Coal Board, the British Railways Board and the Gas Board. In the 1950s the UK saw a slow recovery, most of the "UK industries were nationalised out of necessity",[31] allowing for a centralised mechanism to plan resources and this nationalistic approach continued long into the aftermath of the war. The UK continued a programme of National Service and, coupled with the Korean War, the 1950s experienced a period of low unemployment, with circa 1 million people unemployed, out of a population of 51 million people. At that time, the cost of welfare was just 4% of GDP and the cost of the military 6.6% of GDP with GDP at a level of £13 billion.[32] In order to pay for the military and welfare needs, higher taxation levies were again imposed, but, with disproportionately low wages being paid by both public and private sector industries, the economic recovery was slow.

It was also during this period that the "Founding Fathers of the European Union" were putting into place mechanisms to unite Europe, which was based on the premise that "a United Europe was essential for world peace" (Fairhurst, 2007) and to accommodate that ethos the European Steel and Coal Community, among other initiatives, was established to regulate the industrial production of those commodities. The rationale was that if the production of steel and coal were organised by one overseeing body, there could never again be a situation in which one European country could hold dominance over the other countries by stockpiling the products in preparation for war against one another.

European countries, including the UK, were also discussing the need to open up the markets for trade. These discussions were in part to align with the ethos of "World Peace" but were also driven in part by the lend-lease agreements that the USA had which France, China, Russia and the UK. The loans that the USA made were predicated on US need to extend its export markets and therefore each of the countries was required to enter into trading arrangements with the USA. The UK owed the USA circa $900 million at that time, $900 million it could not repay (ibid.). The European Trading Area, the Common Market and European Free Trade Area were established during the period of 1948 to 1959.

8 *The historic development of VfM*

Between 1959 and 1960, the level of public spending had increased to 40% of GDP.[33] Major government projects were being commissioned to cover civil works, roads, hospitals, schools and universities and subsidies were being provided for agricultural schemes, industry and health service grants. The early 1960's saw a prosperous time for the UK. The economy was buoyant with low levels of unemployment, wages had risen and spending had increased on current fashions, housing and the fashionable refrigerators, televisions and cars. Going out for meals became an accepted pastime and pop culture was a new scene. There was a significant shift in culture with a relaxation of behaviours, the traditional role of a female as a housewife was changing as it became more common for women to go out to work. However, by the late 1960s the boom was coming to an end. While infrastructure works were commencing, the UK was behind its European and US competitors, the lack of investment during the war period was now stifling the economy. It is also with some concern that, in 1962–63, the PAC uncovered what is now known as the "Ferranti" case, a contract that had been awarded by the Ministry of Defence, from which the contracting entity had gained a 63% profit margin (Public Accounts Committee (UK), 2007). In times of trade deficit, it is either unethical or negligent practice on behalf of the procuring authority to be wasting public money on that scale. As a result of this incident and that of Chevaline (1980) major procurements by the Ministry of Defence were thoroughly scrutinised and, indeed, their powers reduced in terms of value of contracts that they were allowed to award without parliamentary oversight.[34] There was still unrest within the industrial sectors and it is said that the UK lacked competitiveness or was it simply the UK lacked the means to become competitive at this time and, consequently, the 1960s saw trade deficits (Chantril, 2018).

In 1972 the UK, while it had a number of local government acts on its statute books governing how the public sector could and could not conduct itself, there was very little legislation set out in terms of how its national and local governments could carry out their purchasing in spite of the Public Accounts Committee's influence and reporting processes. When the UK executed the Single European Act (1972), both national and local governments were required to ensure that the legislative provisions of the European Treaties, Directives and Regulations were incorporated into statute. The provisions of the EEC (now EU) legislation were found to achieve the overarching principles the promotion of fair, transparent and equal opportunities for cross-border trading. This included the promotion of the freedom to provide works, services, supplies and goods among and within each of the member states. Such requirements being the fundamental ethos of being able to grow and encourage economic growth among the member countries by virtue of the opening up of competitive markets and competition being held as a self-policing mechanism to control market forces: an ideal strongly advocated by the future Conservative government (1979).

The historic development of VfM 9

Consumerism was now developing in the UK, with more choices being available to those who could afford to make the choices. Not only could you purchase white goods, but competition meant that there was a choice of where and from whom the population bought the goods and if product a were cheaper in store x, then store y would need to do something to entice the consumer to purchase the product there instead. Thus variances in prices and quality began; personal circumstances, beliefs and need suddenly became part of the purchasing experience. This freedom of choice and growth in consumerism is potentially where society and the general public now require the ability to get the best deal possible for the available money.

While the concept of VfM can be seen to extend at this juncture, it is still not a requirement for the public sector to achieve the ideal in its dealings. In terms of public sector purchasing, it is acknowledged that there was a need for statutory intervention to compel public sector bodies to open up their contracts to the wider market. It is believed that, at the outset, the EU in this regard was a toothless tiger and as such remained inactive and stagnant through to the 1980s because of a lack of power to achieve many of the Treaty provisions.[35] On that basis, the UK had already commenced implementing its own methods in pursuance of its privatisation agenda but, initially at least, nothing in the UK changed.

Its nationalised industries carried on as normal in their purchasing practices. The Public Accounts Committee had already mandated in 1911 that competitive tendering should be undertaken in purchasing on behalf of the public sector but to little avail and, in any event, this mandate did not include the requirement to advertise such opportunities across the borders of the EU member states, in spite of the fact that it had been stated that the country needed to review its dealings with other countries in terms of trade.

Further competition acts began to be introduced, which dictated both to the public and private sectors how business should be conducted to ensure that the EU Treaty principles of transparency and fair treatment in cross-border trading were implemented. For public sector entities, this meant that their purchasing activities were to undergo a significant change.

Initially, this was addressed by the implementation of the Local Government Act 1972, which among other provisions governed how local government should conduct itself. It is also statutorily required local government to put contracts out to tender. This legislation remains the backbone of how local authorities conduct business today.

Society and economy: the influence of the EU 1972–2018

Significantly, the introduction of the EU legislation also coincided with the further political and socioeconomic unrest of the UK. The 1970s had seen a wave of changes in the powers of the trade unions as a movement and voice of the workers; the unions had progressively strengthened and organised since the 1920s and from within the nationalised industries they were now a political strength, which sat in collaboration with the prominent left-wing

10 The historic development of VfM

labour movement of the UK. Their influence and power saw the instigation of the miners' strikes in 1972, 1974 and (most noteworthy) in 1978/79, which became known as the "winter of discontent". This strike action inconvenienced the whole of the UK, leading to mass unrest among the electorate and, as a consequence, a general election was called, from which the political direction of the UK changed towards the first female prime minister. This saw the beginning of Thatcherism in the UK.[36]

The Thatcher government introduced some far-reaching policies that had a dramatic and lasting influence on the UK and its economic position within an ever increasing and competitive worldwide economy.

Privatisation of public services was one such policy that sat within the Thatcher Conservative government's free market policies. These included "trade liberalisation, deregulation, breaking the powers of unions and creating an enterprise culture".[37] The shift in the economic basis of the UK away from being a society dependent on its nationalised and manufacturing industries, to an economy based on a services sector and market economy, was the main thrust of this privatisation policy. The UK needed to be turned into a 21st- Century competitive market economy.

As a result of the changes, many areas within the UK were left bereft of industry, with no form of replacement opportunity. The 1980s' riots and strikes were the result of increasing unemployment with decreasing employment opportunities. It was also at this time that recognition was given to the fact that the construction industry was underachieving. It is, therefore, not surprising that public sector spending reached an all-time high at 45% against GDP (Chantril, 2018).

Unfortunately, the government ideal or expectation from privatisation process was that the private sector would be able to provide employment to those people who suddenly became unemployed; yet, in reality, this was not going to be possible. Low skilled and manual workers would not be in a position to immediately pick up the baton and make the transition into a services sector economy without a significant amount of help "the absence of or excessive withdrawal of the state does not automatically lead to the sustainable development of, or the creation of a private sector" (Hutton, 1995). Not only were the traditional nationalised industries being privatised; public sector, particularly local authorities were heavily criticised for being inefficient, incompetent and nepotistic in their dealings (Bennett & Cirrell, 2009). Local authorities, not unlike nationalised industries, tended to operate on a closed-shop basis that often relied on their in-house teams to provide the services, works that were needed. The Thatcher government introduced in the late 1980s a system of compulsory competitive tendering (CCT), but a lack of experience in tendering and competing within a market economy, meant that the imposed processes were inadequately carried out and often met with resistance and a "public sector rage" (ibid.). Initially, it is believed that these provisions were predominantly ignored and subsequently a raft of legislation appeared to enforce the competitive requirements. Intrinsically, the legislative provisions that were implemented were borne from the requirement to achieve a competitive arena and the VfM "overlap" was nothing more than a by-product of the *"requirement to ensure transparency, level playing fields and cross border competition"* (Arrowsmith, 2005). It is noted that, within the legislative provisions, there is no direct concern with VfM, simply the extension to the requirement to carry out a competitive process and to market test. The legislation neither provides a VfM analysis nor a VfM definition.

While Arrowsmith (1996) expressly provides that the initial CCT requirement was to be carried out to ensure that the in-house provision offered best value for money, the later legislative provisions support a previous assertion from Arrowsmith, namely, that the achievement of VfM was a secondary consequence to undertaking a competitive exercise. The term "best value for money" does not appear within the legislative drafting and indeed does not appear as a legislative-defined term until 1999 and the Local Government Act of that year. Local Authorities were now statutorily required to "secure continuous improvement in the way in which its functions are exercised, having regard to a combination of economy, efficiency and effectiveness" (LGA 1999, section 3[1]), this definition being the only one entrenched within statute.

It is evident that the 1970s, 1980s and 1990s saw significant milestones in terms of entrenching the need for government to be more accountable in terms of public spending within statute, but in terms of defining the concept of VfM or establishing a mechanism from which to track whether it is being achieved or not was still a long way from fruition.

The above notwithstanding, it was also the case in the 1980s that there was a further government investigation into the DeLorean project, this project having been held by the PAC "to have been the gravest example of the mismanagement of public funds, from which a sum of £8.8million was a key issue in an alleged fraud" (Public Accounts Committee (UK), 2007). Thus it could also be argued that the further need to legislate in these terms was as a further step to combat corruption. However, the Public Works, Supplies, Services and Utilities Regulations were introduced by the EU, which, for the first time, not only compelled member states to carry out a tendering process, they also set out prescriptively how the tendering procedures should be carried out to ensure that a level playing field was being maintained across all member state, transparency of dealings as between each tenderer being of paramount importance. Once implemented into the UK procedures these Regulations changed the face of public procurement forever.

This new legislation was a culture shock to the public sector: in spite of the CCT provisions, this new wave of tendering was believed to be restrictive, time consuming and inefficient. However, the introduction of the new processes was timely. Public spending in the 1980s and 1990s also needed to increase again, inflation had become a problem as the UK had entered the European Monetary Union, the Maastricht Treaty and the Exchange Rate Mechanism (ERM) and, in so doing, was required to maintain a 4% rate of inflation, which was proving impossible and, as the country tried to balance its books, a recession hit the UK (Chantril, 2018). Of particular significance

12 *The historic development of VfM*

was the requirement for the government to increase its borrowing, directly as a result of the above societal problems. Black Wednesday (16 September 1992) was the day on which the UK finally removed itself from the ERM. Public spending at this time was again at a high of 45% of GDP (ibid.). This rise in public sector spending now was not only to cover the cost of welfare, national debt and other societal needs arising from the public sector privatisation policies, it was also the time when Treasury introduced a new mechanism to advance public sector infrastructure projects through public–private partnerships in the form of Private Finance Initiatives. It is at this juncture when VfM in the UK appears to develop a further impetus and the beginning of Treasury Green Books, Orange Books and Brown Books all dictating how this should be achieved and the testing mechanism by which it should be measured.

The achievement of VfM within these projects lay at the heart of their procurement. In addition to all of the economic elements, the societal position of the 1980s and 1990s was not a particularly stable time, the economy fluctuated rapidly between boom and bust and back again; however, the new phenomenon developing was that of "old age" and having a system in place to respond to the ever increasing needs of the age of the population; life expectancy over the generations has increased significantly. The statistics produced by the UK Office of National Statistics indicate that a male living in the 1920s would achieve an average age of 55.6 years and a female an average age of 59.6. By the 1980s, this compared to life expectancy having increased to an average age of 71 and 77 years respectively for males and females. In 2018 the figures increased again giving an age range of 80 and 83 years respectively: the population on average is currently living 24.4 years longer now than it did in 1920.[38]

The impact on public expenditure to accommodate the growing demands on the health service, housing and other welfare and social needs to address this increase in population has been phenomenal. Indeed, as a comparator, in 1860 public expenditure was £87 million (circa £8 billion in 2018 terms); by 2019 the level of public expenditure will be £817.5 billion, being 49% of GDP. In 2019 government revenue income is predicted to be in the region of £598.5 billion, some £219 billion deficit.[39]

The impact of such an increase in public spending has many facets, first, there must be an increase in taxation of the public to provide the service and, second, there has to be more wealth creation to ensure that there is sufficient means for the public to pay the taxes being levied. From an ongoing perspective, there has to be heightened scrutiny in how government is spending its money to reduce wastage and it is this backdrop that is part of the driving force for government to achieve VfM. However, there are numerous factors beyond the socioeconomic and legal parameters that drive not only governments to achieve VfM in their projects, but also other stakeholders to other projects.

China

Overview

China's commercial development, not unlike that of the UK, is steeped in a rich political and socioeconomic history dating back centuries. Many emperors and dynasties have carved out Chinese history and culture. The country is geographically the third largest in the world and it could boast the position of being the largest economy in the world during the 13th and 17th Centuries:[40] however, as with all other countries, myriad wars, internal conflicts and disasters deprived China of that status in the world for many years as it regressed into an underdeveloped country with significant wealth gaps.[41] China has, however, undergone a huge transition and once again is becoming increasingly dominant within the worldwide economy currently sitting as the second largest economy globally.[42] This developing economy has also given rise to the introduction of new modes of government, with decentralised local governments and a move away from traditional Chinese ideological governance theories to transparently audited systems of government. This change highlighting the need to achieve value for money, but with a different focus from that of the UK.[43]

China has slowly changed from a state-governed economy to a mixed state and market economy, not dissimilar to the transition experienced by the UK in the 1970s. However, the difference between the UK and China in this regard is that the UK advocates a free and fluctuating market economy whereas China's market economy was described as a state-guided market economy or a Leninist economy, which central state intervention included among other things setting pricing structures within nationalised industry and commercially among traders.[44] The very nature of price fixing at any level acts to distort economies and does not provide a VfM solution.

In order to advance China's socioeconomic transition, there was a need to facilitate political change not just in terms of taking steps towards a free market economy but also in terms of advocating a transparent government. Irrespective of the political control China utilises within its economy, China has begun to flourish economically and, in so doing, not unlike its western counterparts it has encountered socioeconomic problems associated with that transition including migration from the outlying regions of the country into areas where new work is emerging.[45] Historically, this is not the first time that China has had to deal with migrating workforces. However, this migration has put greater pressures on the Chinese government to manage its affairs better. Internal conflict has arisen as calls for government transparency have been made from both global organisations investing and undertaking infrastructure projects, and from the indigenous population who have undergone tremendous socioeconomic changes.[46] Governance and transparency are beginning to improve and budgetary controls and a system of audit are increasing as systems of finance and financial support are

14 The historic development of VfM

crossing into the different regions of China, and also to and from other countries worldwide for myriad reasons. Unlike the UK, however, the system of audit has a focus on the personnel working in public sector organisations, rather than scrutiny of discrete projects.

China has a need to support its continued economic growth to cement its emerging status and build on its reputation within a worldwide market, therefore it has no option but to implement budgetary and financial controls and modernise its system of government, which has been developing since 1520 BC.[47] While China now works within the remit of the UNCITRAL Model Law provisions in procurement, establishing fairness in its dealings with contractors, it remains the case that within China's provincial governments there is a reluctance to accede to the calls for transparency, in spite of this being a central government requirement and a fundamental provision within the UNCITRAL doctrine. It remains the position that the legislature advocates a different picture, the People's Republic of China Law of Safeguarding State Secrecy is evidenced within academic debate that this piece of widely drafted legislation has fettered progress in this respect, particularly when trying to obtain information from the government. It is said that the wide drafting of the legislation allows officers the discretion to determine what does or does not constitute a state secret.[48] The Chinese Supreme Court has shown support and offered more legal protection for the "public right to know" in its judgments, but it is said that the only way to truly show that China supports transparency is to effectively amend its State Secrecy Laws. Transparency and public accountability of government affairs is known to be the foundation for efficient, effective and responsible government. The developing Chinese Audit Office, however, has increased its levels of transparency and publicises its reports electronically.[49]

VfM in China has not advanced through the same hoops as that of its UK comparator. Indeed, when VFM first emerges in China it is through the introduction of a system of audit being implemented by government to monitor the decentralised behaviour of local governments and their officials, circa 1970 (ibid.). This lack of interest in VfM in the early years can also arguably be linked to the state interventionist policies, price fixing and communist principles of "everyone being the same" living in communes, without the freedom of choice or a competitive market to provide that choice. However, VFM is becoming an important requirement within the Chinese auditing processes, arguably as a need to "control extravagant position related consumerism" and curb the corruption that has blighted the reputation of China for a number of decades. It is not therefore surprising that VfM testing and auditing is carried out against individuals.

In any event, it appears that the concept relating to VfM when considering infrastructure also refers to effectiveness, efficiency and cost control or economy, described as the 3Es by Gong (2009). Evidence suggests that the VfM concept in China does not as yet take on the wider nontangible and subjective qualitative elements incorporated into the UK definition. In 2004 Infrastructure

UK provided a report to China setting out a suggested procurement process for PPP collaboration projects within which it advises the use of the Public/Private Sector Comparator to compare the VfM process. This seems odd advice based on the fact that, by 2004, the UK had moved away from using the simple PSC test and that China through its own economic and government evolution has identified that VfM was a "performance audit" mechanism.

Politics, society and economy: the early years

While, as we have identified above, the concept of VfM does not arise in China until the 1990s, it is important to consider the socio-political growth of China to understand why. The Shang Dynasty, being the first recorded Dynasty to rule China (1520–1030 BC) developed China's copper mining industry and expanded into the Chinese landscape to advance its regions. During this period the Shang built up good trading relationships with the rest of mainland Asia.[50] However, in 1030 BC, the Chou Dynasty took over the Shang Territory and ruled until circa 770 BC. The Chou were responsible for the establishment of the first system of rulers,[51] this system not being that dissimilar to the feudal system adopted by the UK. Market systems operated and currencies were used but were regional and often coins from one region were deemed to be inferior to those from another region, on that basis, therefore, there had been a judgement made in terms of the value of money (based on the weight of the coin).[52] There is no indication in the reading as to what the value for money might be equated to at this time.

From 475 BC to 221BC the Chou were in almost constant conflict, which resulted in a long period of socioeconomic and political instability within their regions, however, during this period huge advancements were made: they were responsible for the first developed system of writing, bronze was used for tools and animals utilised for the first time in the production of agricultural crops. Daoism, Confucianism and legalism emerged as significant academic and philosophical schools of thought. Public administration was being developed along the lines of Confucianism and political ideologies, but the changing dynasties had a significant development impact on the Chinese socio-political landscape (ibid.).

The Chin Dynasty arose during this period of warring (221–207 BC) and they were ultimately responsible for the unification of China and ruled on the basis of the rule of law.

The Han Dynasty (207BC–220AD, incorporating both periods of rule) were the next dynasty to make significant changes: they replaced the penal code introduced by the Chin by reintroducing the previous feudal system and then further developing that system into a central government with regional administrations, which were further divided into districts and hamlets. The administrations were staffed by administrators on the basis of benevolent rule and good statesmanship. Confucius was the driving force behind this regime, albeit that there remained the influence of the rule of law and the penal code of the Chin. He further developed a system of schooling for anyone seeking to take office. This system developed into quite an educational hurdle; as time progressed

16   *The historic development of VfM*

anyone seeking office in the government must have been educated in the ways of Confucius to an equivalent of degree standard. The roles were also restricted to try to prevent corruption becoming entrenched and it was not possible to employ relatives or persons connected through marriage. This system of governance and the process of education can be said to have been quite advanced for its time. This was further extended to ensure that administrative officers did not hold a position for more than a three-year period and they could not be assigned to the districts from where they originated.[53]

The Han Dynasty was also responsible for developing roads and transport infrastructure to open up the Silk Route, which is said to have transported silk to as far away as the Roman Empire. This trading route was one of the most successful of the time and gave China an advanced position in terms of being a worldwide trading hub (Overy, 2011). It was also during this period that there was a significant growth in the money economy and nationalisation of industry to pay for the war efforts private mints were closed during the Han Dynasty in favour of a centralised mint in 113BC. The distribution of currency was to be overseen by the Minister of Finance, which also oversaw the collection of taxes. The taxation system fluctuated heavily during this period as concessions were granted to peasant farmers. Hired labour began to increase and state pricing intervention was reduced during the Han period as business environments began to develop in conjunction with county administration initiatives. While the growth in administration and business continued, there was no mechanism under which financial scrutiny or controls were performed. The Han Dynasty came to an end with the abdication of the Han Emperor, and from 220AD China was catapulted into what has been described as a further long period of warring, which again fragmented China (ibid.).

Political, social and economic instability followed until China was reunified under the Sui Dynasty (581–618 AD). The Suis were responsible for a number of infrastructure projects and further economic growth in spite of a number of territorial advances by warring factions. The Suis maintained the complex system of bureaucracy and maintained the local administrative structures; land, however was divided into smaller plots as the country was heading towards bankruptcy.[54]

In the years 618–907, the T'ang Dynasty ruled, which was held to be the "Golden Age" of China as arts, poetry and culture thrived, military power advanced and economic prosperity prevailed. From this period of prosperity, China fell into political disarray for a period of 50 years until the succeeding of the Song Dynasty, which pulled the political and economic environment of China back into a new golden age. The Songs were held to be "a super power, with a vibrant market economy with a flourishing global trade" they were also known to have "had an extraordinary amount of money in circulation", the amount of renminbi (RMB) in circulation at that time being in the region of 260 billion coins. Even with this amount of currency in circulation, it is stated that the economy remained stable, barring one or two war disruptions, for almost one and a half centuries (ibid.)

The historic development of VfM   17

However, the Mongols invaded China in the early 13th Century under the rule of Kublai Khan, which spiralled China into a period of instability and turmoil. This was not recovered until the Ming Dynasty put the economy back on track during 1279–1368 and through the Ming period China again peaked as a superpower both in terms of sea power and economy. The Ming Dynasty prevailed until 1644, introducing further taxation, however, alleged corruption, crop failures, internal uprisings and invasions led to the eventual downfall of the Ming to be replaced by the Ch'ing Dynasty, which ruled until 1911. While the Ch'ing initially grew the economic prosperity of China, an economic crisis was on the horizon. Population growth could not be sustained and peasant revolts happened on a regular basis. Widespread corruption within the administration meant that the system of government was ineffective and by the 1830s foreign intervention and expansion was increasing, the Opium Wars took a huge toll on the Chinese economy until devastation hit as China collapsed and the imperial system ended in revolution in 1911.[55]

Politics, society and economy: WWI (1914–1918) and its aftermath

WWI has been held as the war that was the turning point for China on a global scale, in spite of China's having declared itself a neutral state because of the partial colonisation of the country by the many different European nations. However, Japanese involvement in the war and the striking of a Chinese ship by a German U-boat, which killed an estimated 1,950 Chinese civilians, saw China enter the war. The Chinese were further encouraged through other financial incentives from Japan and the USA to changing its neutral status against Germany. By participating in the war, the Chinese had envisaged that they would be able to reclaim territories that had been taken by Germany. WWI is also debated as being the period of time within Chinese history that a new proletariat was being formed, moving away from the Confucianism politics of old. By the end of the war, and progressing into the 1920s, China began to allow emigration for its nationals, which allowed them to learn about the new technologies that were available on the global market and be schooled in European and western environments, thus setting the foundations to enable the future development and reform of Chinese society. It was, however, during the 1920s and China's period of cultural and intellectual growth that China changed from a monarchy into a republic.[56]

Economically, China gained from the war as it opened up import opportunities for Chinese merchants and entrepreneurs. The requirement for the export from China for raw materials and food meant that China gained a bigger proportion of international trade, which the USA encouraged. However, at the end of the war, the Chinese had not achieved what it had hoped in terms of liberalisation of its territories from foreign rule, indeed the Versailles Treaty entrenched foreign dictat into their provinces even further.[57] Ultimately, this gave rise to the socialist movement taking the political strength as

18   *The historic development of VfM*

the Chinese viewed the imperialist west with distrust[58] (Muhlhahn, Klaus). This nationalist approach did not focus its mind on achieving value for money; indeed, during this period the focus turned to commune-based lifestyles and the distribution of food to address the social problems that the country was facing with shortages of food. The war had required a significant export of the basic foods away from the China to the western world to feed the troops and drought brought about a 12-month period of famine. These conditions were to be faced again with the onset of WWII when China again was called on to provide grain to the troops (BBC History, 2018).

Politics, society and economy: WWII (1939–1945) and its aftermath

China contributed significantly to WWII, not unlike every other country that participated; the loss of life was reported to be in the region of 14 million and the displacement of Chinese nationals was significant. However, relations between the USA and Chinese were strained. The famine that had overtaken in China in 1942 was alleged to have arisen as a result of corruption and political mismanagement by the nationalists. A period of political unrest continued as the country divided and civil war broke out between the Communist Party of China and the Nationalist Party of China, unrest that ended only in 1950. The formation of the People's Republic of China took control of mainland China with the Republic of China controlling Taiwan. Economically, during the civil war, Chinese GDP was very low, there were high rates of unemployment and high levels of inflation. In conjunction with this backdrop, there was also a food shortage, giving rise to malnutrition. Land had been organised along the lines of a feudal system and as these feudal lords were disposed by the communist regime and a centralised restructuring programme commenced; the impact of this was that the economy began to improve. The drive forward at this time was to reduce corruption, extravagance and bureaucracy and to develop the economy. China became known as one of the most egalitarian states of its time. Yet the growth of the state and the advancements of the economy did not see a reduction in bureaucracy as government indeed grew and as taxation grew so it is alleged that wide-scale corruption grew. In response to the growing problems this regime was creating, the Chinese solution as part of its Great Leap Forward plan (1958) was to develop communes under the control of the government with land being collectivised during 1958, the intention of the commune being to redistribute food, and control resources However, this great plan failed and resulted in famine in 1961.[59]

Politics, society and economy: 1960s–1972

The following decade, from 1961 to 1971, there was continued unrest, poverty was rife and only sporadic advancements in technology as communism under Mao held the country back significantly. Mao's death in 1976 saw him replaced by Deng Xiaoping who spearheaded a decision to pursue the "Four Modernisations" (agriculture, industry, national defence and science and technology).[60] The drive was to achieve material prosperity. Market reforms were initiated in 1978, again moving control from a centrally planned economy to a market-based structure. This shift resulted in very rapid social and economic growth, which was held to have lifted more than 800 million people out of poverty. The total population count at that time was in the region of 1.3 billion people. The economic reform of this time highlighted that there was a need to introduce audit controls and mechanisms for financial scrutiny to assist in the plan to move towards efficiency, autonomy and competition. Such auditing mechanisms would allow decentralised local economies to be effectively supervised.[61]

Politics, society and economy: the influence of the EU 1972–2018

Further policies of "retrenchment" in the 1980s stabilised the economy, but there was still socio-political unrest and, even though by 1982 the constitution of China gave legal mandate for the supervision of the national financial and monetary use through the Chinese National Audit Office, which was established in 1983, corruption in public office was still a concern. The focus at this point being on state-owned enterprises, they were it is stated constantly showing a loss, estimated around RMB 40.9 billion, the fear of a downward economic spiral combined with the Tiananmen Square protest in 1989 and the horrific gunning down of students by military forces were atrocities seen around the globe. China's relationship internationally was significantly damaged as a result of this state action. Impetus, therefore, was the further introduction of legislative provisions that called for transparency and deeper and more efficient scrutiny. More thorough market reforms were seen in the 1990s, as the rest of the world had China on its radar.

By 2000 China had systematic anti-corruption activities entrenched within its economic practices, which were highlighted in 2000 when the former deputy chairman of the People's Congress was executed for taking bribes. By 2001 China were developing progressively, becoming members of the World Trade Organisation (WTO) and subsequently awarded the hosting of the 2008 Olympic Games. In becoming a member of the WTO, it elected to subscribe to the rules relating to procurement under that trading organisation, which called for transparent, and fair systems to be developed in procuring public sector infrastructure projects. In reviewing the Chinese regulatory framework within which it is required to work when procuring contracts on behalf of the government the predominant principles that are advocated are those based on transparency, openness, fair competition, impartiality and honesty. The focus on such issues being primarily to address the corruption that had become prevalent and the extravagant purchasing of the statesmen. This combined with the Chinese system of

20 *The historic development of VfM*

economically responsibility auditing seems to suggest that it is not only the projects in China that are audited, but the officers responsible for delivering such projects are also subject to a detailed audit process driving China's VfM accountability position.[62]

Further advances in the procurement regulations the People's Republic of China apply are linked to further development of small and medium enterprises in technology, the environment in terms of its Green Agenda. Its links with the United Nations also promote the new projects that China is taking forward into the future, such developments include the reopening of the Silk Route and further investments at home and abroad securing its place in the future economy on a worldwide scale. The World Bank confirms that China has been the largest contributor to world growth since 2008 with future goals identified up to 2030. However, the major concern on the horizon appears to be China's financial markets, which have been identified as being in a position akin to the one in the USA and the UK in 2008, which resulted in the financial crisis at that time. Hopefully, the lessons from the USA and the UK can be deployed to avert such an event, if not the global repercussions could once again be significant economically.

Australia

Overview

Australia does not have such a varied depth of public administrative history as that of its comparators within this chapter, therefore, its situation in terms of its legal, political socioeconomic development differs fundamentally, however, there are some similarities in historical events that evidence how socioeconomic changes impact on societal views in terms of public policy and the understanding of "public value".

Australia was first discovered in 1606 by the Dutch, with its indigenous Aboriginal people being described as a simple race although the Dutch and British explorers could not agree whether they were a happy or miserable population.[63] The Aboriginals had existed and inhabited Australia in the region of 70,000 years prior to that time. They fed off the land sustainably catering simply for their needs in a hunter-gather lifestyle and respecting their environment. It is said that they stopped hunting seasonally to allow regrowth of their food supplies. Their beliefs were predominantly spiritual, the spiritual ethos forming the rules of the land from which they lived. Their social structure was based on a structure of alliances between different clans. It is said that they lived by a code of "intricate kinship rules" presided over by meetings and rituals to maintain order between the clans and domestic life. They used stone, wood and fire as their main tools for survival and lived in huts in food-rich areas with some of the clans adopting a nomadic existence. Their population held to have been in the region of 750,000,000 people.[64]

The Aboriginals' first encounter with western culture seemed uneventful as the Dutch landed in 1688 but determined that the land had no use for them.[65] However, the UK, through the discovery of Australia in 1788, determined that Australia would be a useful base for extending its trade links with China and that it would be an ideal place, having an over-populated prison system in the UK, to use as a penal colony. New South Wales and Tasmania were both used as such until 1850.[66]

The Aboriginals suffered dramatically through this period, conflict with westerners over land ensued, wars were carried out based on guerrilla warfare which continued until 1837 and beyond, many atrocities inflicted on the Aboriginals by the British and the exposure to western illnesses also meant that the Aboriginal population reduced significantly. In 1837 a British select committee established a somewhat misnamed "policy of protection" for the Aboriginals, but this did not stop the killings. A further board for the protection of Aboriginals was established, empowering the removal of Aboriginal children from their families, with the aim of sending them to public schools. By 1883 the protection board had the power to segregate the Aboriginals as part of this warped protection policy.[67]

Amid this chaos, Australia began to develop commercially. Its early settlers relied heavily on the commissionaires as the supplier of goods and money while the penal regime was being operated. In order to support this system, a private economy began to emerge. Land grants were given to senior officials and prisoners who had served their time and it was soon realised that the prisoners had skills that would assist in the development of the colonies, such as tradesmen, clerks, labourers and craftsmen. The economy began to develop around European and British needs for export and increasingly included the export of wool. Immigration was soon needed to feed to the expansion of the economy and British citizens made the move over. The economy was therefore founded and developed on the socio-political and legal principles of the UK. Rural growth continued and the Gold Rush in 1851 provided further impetus within the socioeconomic development of Australia. This discovery brought immigrants from other countries and not just the UK.

While the value of gold at this time was more significant than value for money, the Gold Rush led to an increase in population and the creation of wealth. However, land continued to be taken from the Aboriginals with massacres and conflict continuing up to and throughout the 1900s.

The influx of immigrants to take advantage of the Gold Rush also meant that the Australian population was increasing, requiring basic infrastructure to be developed. However, the Australian landscape by its very nature is harsh and unrelenting and, while technological advances were being made, it was virtually impossible to traverse a continent of such a diverse and vast terrain. The onset of drought from the mid-1890s to 1903 also had a significant economic impact,

22 *The historic development of VfM*

particularly of the farming industry, but technological advances meant that some rural industries still continued to develop.

In spite of the external influences, the Australian federal and state governments continued their persecution of the Aboriginals. In 1934 Aboriginals were granted the right to cease being Aboriginal to enable them to have the same rights as the whites, but the policy of removing children from homes continued and the programme to "de-Aboriginalise" the Aboriginals continued into the 1960s.[68] By 1965 integration policies were beginning to appear, but they were still predominantly biased and it was not until the 1970s that Aboriginals were allowed to establish their homes back into their homelands and the White Australia Policy abolished, with the statement that "when migration began on the 26th January 1788 all Australians were black and the first migrants were white and not very well selected" (Al Grassby, Minister for Immigration 1972–1974). The transition processes are still taking place (2018), apologies are being given and the Aboriginal history is now being taught in schools within Australia. Such abhorrent events did not prevent Australia from growing commercially.

Politics, society and economy: the early years

By 1900 Australia was being described as the "working man's paradise" because of the wealth generated predominantly by the agricultural industry. The separate colonies of Australia federated into the Commonwealth of Australia in 1901.[69] Australia at this time still depended on the UK for its finance, labour and trading markets. Australia's connection with the UK continued for many years. The foundations of the government of Australia were born in 1901 when the six self-governing colonies, now the six states of Australia, agreed and ratified a central constitution with Queen Elizabeth II of England (confusingly also referred to as the Queen of Australia) being the official head of state. The Queen of Australia is represented by the governor general of Australia with executive powers delegated by the constitution to the Australian prime minister. The system of government is not dissimilar to that of the UK, but has similarities within it from the USA as the houses of parliament are separated into two distinct houses: the senate and the house of representatives as the Commonwealth government.[70] Emitting from that, the six states each then has its own sovereign parliament, with the High Court of Australia presiding over the six areas. The next level of government is a system of local government akin to that of the UK, which represents the individual shires, towns and cities through elected councillors. The government process is divided into the legislature, executive and judiciary, again akin to that of the UK, which operates on the basis of the principle of the separation of powers. State intervention into people's lives in Australia is not as far reaching as that of the UK. Indeed, unemployment benefit was not available until 1988 with a further review being undertaken in 2000.

While some healthcare had been available since 1788, general public health units were not introduced until 1990 to protect and monitor health at

The historic development of VfM   23

more local level. However, these units did not provide a completely free service. Taxation on trade barriers had been in existence in Australia since 1813, but this system was used as a mechanism to erect trade barriers between each of the states. The major trading items at that time being timber, wool, whale oil and seal skins. Early taxation was to provide orphanages, infrastructure within Sydney, goals and hospital equipment. The Gold Rush also provided an opportunity for further taxations to be imposed through a licensing system for mines. However, as with many other developing countries, the taxation system and the share of the wealth were inequitable. This led to rebellions, as the main socioeconomic and political divide at this time was the protectionism as between each of the Australian states. The introduction of the federated government changed this position, but this did not stop taxation, indeed, additional taxation was introduced to pay for public services. However, this was not introduced until 1909 and it remained the position that the service was not entirely free. The need for change was driven more from a need to pay for the administrative resource required by each of the individual states at this time more than for any other issue.

Politics, society and economy: WWI (1914–1918) and its aftermath

Australia's involvement in WWI was unconditional, with its links to the UK being the driving force of this commitment. In spite of its having only a very small population, it sent to the front line a significant number of forces combined with those men from New Zealand (later to be known as the ANZACs). It is held that WWI put Australia on a global map as an independent country in its own right, however, because its economy was so closely dependent on trade with the UK, when the UK went into depression in the aftermath of the war, so did Australia. Unemployment reached 32% of the population and Australia suffered economically; the war casualties were vast and when the wounded soldiers returned home, there was an epidemic Spanish flu, which cost the Australian population another 12,000 lives. The cost of medical treatment, pensions and welfare escalated to enormous proportions, putting a significant strain on the economy. Fiscal policies were put into place to alleviate the depression, some of which were protectionist, including increasing in tariffs for imports. However, the dependence on the UK remained and stimulus packages were provided from the UK. While such stimulus was being provided it is also at this time that the system of taxation was again being changed, this time to accommodate the costs of welfare and social care and war effort. It was with these costs that income tax was introduced in Australia in 1915. Between the wars the taxation system increased its revenue on both a state and federal level and complex systems akin to that of the UK began to develop. Industrial disputes began to characterise the political environment of Australia in the 1920s, the aim of which was to improve working conditions for the working-class population, as with

24 The historic development of VfM

the UK the new goods that were becoming available from the USA were also becoming available within Australia, again a wealth divide meant that not everyone benefitted. In order to boost the economy at the time, Australia looked to the UK for trade deals, loans and again importation of labour. The overreliance on the UK, however, meant that when the UK headed into depression in the 1930s so did Australia. Australia's depression, however, ended in 1932. By the mid-1930s Australia started to increase its spending on its armed forces. It was concerned that there was increased aggression by Japan in China and increased concerns around Hitler's advances.

Politics, society and economy: WWII (1939–1945) and its aftermath

The Australian Prime Minister at the time, Robert Menzies, informed the citizens of Australia on 3 September 1939 that as the UK had declared war on Germany and, in the face of that news, it was now also the case that Australia was doing the same. The war effort was difficult for Australia, which was committed to the battle in Europe, but, at the same time, knew that the battles being fought in the Pacific by the Japanese were or should have been of more significance to the Australians. The Pearl Harbor attack by the Japanese proved the Australian assertion to be correct and from that point, it pledged its support of the US troops unfettered by its historical links to the UK. Australian losses were again heavy in terms of lives and infrastructure during World War II.

In the aftermath of the war, Australia relaunched its policy of colonisation, in which it offered assisted travel to Europeans from Greece, the UK and other areas to take up residence in Australia to repopulate the country and to rebuild the economy. By 1942 austerity and rationing had been introduced and in order to ensure that Australia grew uniform tax laws were introduced across the states, which were from that point onwards controlled and regulated by the federal government.

Politics, society and economy: 1960s–1972

The White Australia Policy was dismantled and the biggest social and political policy during this time was to return stolen land back to the Aboriginal clans and to provide compensation for the children who had been stolen from their families. Australia wanted to show that this was a country where everyone could have a "fair go". Not unlike its UK counterparts, the 1960s saw much social and economic change, with the introduction of rock and roll, the arrival of the television. Menzies, who was the Prime Minister during this period, was a strong supporter of the Commonwealth, although he extended trade links with both the USA and with Japan. Indeed, Japan soon became Australia's biggest trading partner. There was a further call for re-colonisation of Australia from Europe and assisted package deals were offered to those who wanted to re-establish in Australia. For a payment of

The historic development of VfM   25

£10 per person and commitment of two years, passage to Australia was given. All professions, trades and services needed to be established and replenished.

Politics, society and economy: the influence of the EU 1972–2018

Trading relationships with the UK had begun to decrease in the 1950s, but while the Commonwealth still supported Australia, it was believed that the UK's entry into the EU was the UK severing its ties to its Commonwealth families, albeit that Queen Elizabeth II stated that this was not the case. It was expected that tariff concessions that Australian goods benefitted from would be reduced.

Australia developed its system of "new public management" around the 1980s and 1990s as it began to realise that deregulation of the markets and less intervention from the state would increase efficient and cooperative markets.[71] In so doing, it emphasised "managing for results", which has been interpreted to mean "managing to achieve value for money" (Wanna et al). It is debated by Wanna et al. that Australia's budgetary policies had derived from its alignment with the Commonwealth thus giving Australia an advanced and strong focus on monitoring and implementation of scrutiny processes for its financial management assisted in this transition. It is, however, also suggested that performance information is still not the predominant concern and, while Australia has a number of budgetary monitoring systems in place that are generated by the Australian National Audit Office, Wanna et al. express that there is a "manifest leniency about being honest and transparent in terms of Value for Money".[72]

Australia, being such a vast country, is still expanding both economically and in terms of infrastructure developments, particularly road and rail links. In order to progress such projects with finite resources, the Australian government commissioned, as an independent statutory body, Infrastructure Australia, with a mandate to prioritise and progress nationally significant infrastructure. This department, collaboratively with the Department of Infrastructure and Regional Development, follows a stringent assessment framework to determine whether projects should be approved for progression, the majority of which in 2018 relate to the opening up of road and rail links across the different territories of Australia. As part of this assessment framework, in order to prove that a project is VfM in terms of its progression, Australia should use the public sector comparator test as its main assessment with a brief reference to a qualitative measurement relating to public benefit and define VfM accordingly as "a quantitative and qualitative assessment of the costs and benefits of public versus private provision of services".

The ongoing projects in terms of Infrastructure Development, the Australian government confirm that it is committing to investing $76 billion using a combination of grant funding, loans and equity investment from

26 The historic development of VfM

2017–2018 to 2026–2027, to include rail, air and other transport upgrades and developments. With such a spend profile being committed, it is therefore essential that Australia, like the UK, takes steps to recognise the importance of achieving VfM through budgetary scrutiny and transparency, incorporating as necessary such public value tests as identified as being a paradigmatic change to the old form of new public management systems traditionally operated.

South Africa

Overview

Africa has a vast socioeconomic, political and cultural history, pre-dating all other continental civilisations. Yet, so much of this history remains to be found in areas of Africa that are inaccessible as a result of ongoing conflict, this continuing conflict and the outside invasions has debilitated the socioeconomic position of Africa for centuries. It is the second largest continent, which accommodates some 53 independent countries within its boundaries. It sits with its borders in the Mediterranean Sea to the north, the Red Sea to the north-northeast, the Indian Ocean to the east, and to the south and up the West Coast the Atlantic Ocean. It is bisected by the equator dividing the land almost in half, the far north governed climatically by the Tropic of Cancer and the southern half governed climatically by the Tropic of Capricorn, making the land rich in minerals, abundant with diverse agricultural produce in different regions and ensuring that as a trading hub it is very well located.[73]

The North African Egyptians were among the first in history to utilise stone as a tool for agricultural purposes and fishing, evidence also supports that the fact that the early North African people in the seventh millennium BC were adept at animal herding. By 2000 BC, substantial towns were emerging in the northern, central and southern sub-Saharan regions. Climatic changes, however, were forcing migration southwards, which helped the knowledge and technology spread into many different regions by sharing farming and agricultural techniques.

The Roman Empire extended into North Africa by 30 BC, conquering Egypt and, as a consequence, advancement in technology and civilized order were disseminated. By the first millennium BC, it is evident that iron and bronze were being used in the southwestern African territories.[74] This use of iron has been associated with further developments in crop cultivation and animal farming particularly identified in the region of Namibia and the Cape Province at the same time as the Cape potteries are discovered. However, the ancient way of life was of a nomadic culture. During this period of time, trading routes were being forged across the continent and the development of individual states was taking place (ibid.). By the late Middle Ages the kingdoms of western and central Sudan were thriving, universities were being established and allegiances between different states emerging as trading partners. By 1498 when the

Portuguese landed on the west coast of Africa, Africa was already becoming a prosperous continent. Unfortunately, this settlement by the Portuguese and the influx of western cultures had a dramatic impact on Africa, from which it is still trying to recover.

The Portuguese began exporting African nationals as slaves to Brazil, a trend that would impact African prosperity, culture, life and development on an enormous level debilitating its future for decades. The Dutch settlers were next forming the Dutch East India Trading Company (1602) and establishing itself on the east and south coast of Africa at the Cape of Good Hope to become the most strategically placed and formidable trading company. By the 17th Century, the British had established the English East India Trading Company and utilised the area to build up its links to China and access to the Silk Route established to connect to India.[75]

The prosperity of the Dutch, when they settled built up relationships with the Bantu-speaking African states, continued, as did the area around Zimbabwe, which was deemed to be a great religious and political centre with major trade links to China (ibid.). However, as European countries became more involved in Africa, they took more from the economy, particularly slaves, as they needed them to work the mines and plantations of the Americas. It is reported that 11.5 million slaves were taken from Africa during the period 1450 to 1870. Whereas during the same period of time it is recorded that 1.25 million white European slaves were brought into North Africa for use on public works (ibid.).

From the early 18th Century Africa became embroiled in a combination of internal conflict, religious wars and further European invasion: the French invaded Algeria, the British took the Cape from the Dutch and by 1913 the French ruled almost one-third of the continent. European turmoil and conflict continued to debilitate Africa up to and including the Boer Wars ending in 1902 and beyond. By 1909 South Africa became one of the first independent countries within continental Africa, albeit that this was not a time for celebration for South Africa as its troubles were to continue for many more years; but many more states followed in gaining independence sporadically during the 1940s, 50s, 60s and 70s.[76]

While independence across the African states was significant during the 1900s, continuing conflict, drought, political instability, tropical diseases, natural disasters and AIDS blocked Africa's social and economic advancement. Each state had small markets, little in terms of welfare services and public utilities and infrastructure was lacking. At this juncture, there is no consideration of what VfM should be. Widespread corruption, one party rule and successive military struggles for control have all contributed to many failing attempts to stabilise the African economy. It comes therefore as little surprise that the concept of achieving value for money in dealings has not been at the forefront of economic-political or social concern for Africa. It was, however, recognised by the 1930s that government and nationalised industry was bureaucratic, ineffective

28 *The historic development of VfM*

and prone to overspending. The need to achieve efficiencies, develop effective practices and implement cost controls through transparency of dealings is evident, however, such transparency of government was to be a long way in the making.

South Africa, amid the trials and tribulations of Africa, and of its own, has, however, managed to develop as a country and, being the first to gain independence from the British in 1909, it will be the focus of this section, because of its diverse socioeconomic and political history and progress within the worldwide economy.

Politics, society and economy: the early years

South Africa, along with many other countries within continental Africa, had its beginnings tarnished by the invasions and abuse from western countries, from its discovery by western explorers in 1478, the Portuguese.[77] South Africa was christened the Cape of Good Hope by King John II of Portugal because of the "optimism" of having opened up a further trading route to the east and India. The Dutch were soon to follow the Portuguese and settled in 1652 in what is now the city of Cape Town. The area grew tremendously both in population and in size to the north and northeast as Dutch settlers migrated from France to escape persecution. The Dutch East India Trading Company established itself within the territory to supply passing ships with fresh fruit and vegetables that were abundant in the area and, as a result, the Cape saw a further influx of settlers. Economically the town prospered and the settlers were provided land on which to establish their homes, this, it would transpire, was land stolen from South African nationals.

As the French were enemies of the British, it was only a matter of time before the British Navy were to invade the Cape, which it did during the Napoleonic wars. British rule was finally established in South Africa in 1806. The relationships between the Dutch republican farmers (Boers) and the British were also deteriorating as diamonds and gold were discovered further increasing wealth and trading opportunities. A large portion of Boers left the Cape and moved into the nearby areas of the Transvaal and Orange Free State to avoid British rule. This, however, was short lived as the British in 1877 determined to annex the Transvaal territory to control the gold mines expanded taking the territory from the Boers, while initially the Boers adopted a passive resistance to the extension of the British territory; this passive resistance soon turned to armed combat when the British confirmed their intentions to retain the state. It is alleged that the Boer Wars were the bloodiest wars of their time. The first of the two Boer Wars, which are referred to as the War of South Africa, and the Second War of Independence, in order to ensure that the wider world understood that the impact of these wars affected not just the westerners but also the South African population as well and that while this war was described as a white War,

The historic development of VfM   29

many black African people perished. The wars were eventually won by the British in 1902, but that did not pave the way for the economic growth of South Africa.

Even before the Boer Wars the relationships between the black nationals and the white Afrikaner Europeans were very strained, racial discrimination was already entrenched within South Africa. Politically, this division deepened and the African People's Organisation formed in 1902, to represent the interests of the "educated coloured people" but legislative provisions were being enacted that further entrenched the policies of discrimination. The British had envisaged uniting the Boer states, an aim that was realised in 1909 and the Union of South Africa, while this gave independence from the UK, this did not address what has been described in historical documents as the Constitutional Crisis facing South Africa at that time, the segregation of South Africa by the Dutch descendants, the white Afrikaners. This system laid the foundations of apartheid and put in place a system of white rule to "suppress the aspirations of the African communities". Black African communities became marginalised and disaffected. The wealth divide was evident and extremely disproportionate between the white Afrikaners and the black African population who were gradually being dehumanised. Indeed, the divide was further exacerbated in 1913 with the passing of the Natives Land Act, which prevented black South African people from purchasing, leasing or using land, except in designated Bantustans. This disaffection caused further extreme poverty and a strain on small areas of land. The Bantustans neither gave the Black South African people their independence nor did they resolve the need for homes within and around the City of Cape Town, which relied heavily on workers from the communities. This requirement for labour saw the beginning of the establishment of townships, which developed to accommodate the habitation of the black communities.[78]

Politics, society and economy: WWI (1914–1918) and its aftermath

South Africa did not escape involvement in WWI, even though the Union was only four years old at the date of the outbreak. The president saw the war as an opportunity to enable expansion into the German territory annexed to the west of the Union of South Africa. However, this is was not to be the case. Indeed, the political agreements signed at Versailles saw the converse situation arise and the territories further entrenched into European ownership. The war caused disruption to the economic development of South Africa as trade from imported goods reduced, although the gold mines helped prop the economy as the UK agreed to buy the output from the mines that they controlled; but this was not without its problems. The economy was stifled further when an influenza outbreak hit South Africa in 1918. This outbreak led to the implementation of the Public Health Act in

30 *The historic development of VfM*

1919, although it was of limited use. The Public Health Department had little money with which to implement any effective service; instead, it simply advised private employers and other public authorities and any real assistance given was for the benefit of the white population. The squalid conditions within which the black Africans were forced to live were not being addressed.

By 1920 it was understood that there was a need to enforce decent standards of planning, construction, hygiene and sanitation and with a view to addressing this position the Public Health Department established a Central Housing Board. The Housing Act 1920 allowed the launch of a large-scale housing scheme to build new homes and to give power to enforce necessary standards. In accordance with the Act, the government, released money to its local authorities in the form of loans to allow them to build homes. However, by 1930 only 7,609 projects had been undertaken; indeed, it was discovered that Johannesburg had been clearing slum areas, but the authorities were not providing any additional suitable accommodation. Makeshift dwellings were a common feature and were overcrowded and often overrun by vermin, hence, the spread of disease was inevitable. Indeed, even those families who had a dwelling, because the rents were so high, accommodation had to be sublet to family members and overcrowding became a problem.

Other socioeconomic problems facing Africa at this time related to the effects of the worldwide depression, which created further unemployment in South Africa, exacerbated among the black South Africans as white workers took up more of the labour-oriented roles within mines and women entered the labour market.

Issues within the mines became even more extreme, particularly as production needed to be increased. The white workers were becoming resentful of the trend of employing lower skilled and lower paid black workers and, with Chinese workers being imported after WWI, this situation culminated in what has been described as the Rand Revolt in 1922, when a series of strikes led to military action, loss of life and significant cost to the economy. There was also a rise in nationalism among the Afrikaners, who, as a minority ruling regime, were trying through legislative means to entrench their ruling positions and further entrenching the principals of segregation. Examples of the legislative enactments are the Industrial Conciliation Act 1924, the Wages Act and, finally, the Mines and Works Amendments Act 1926, establishing further racial segregation and prohibitions relating to colour in certain mining jobs. While it is evident at this time in South Africa that the government authorities were growing, it is also evident that the economy was not growing sufficiently well to ensure that it could fund the increasing demand for social reform and welfare being demanded by every faction of South Africa. The government had no alternative but to consider what would happen after the war when "it would no longer be just a question of providing the minimum safety net".[79]

The historic development of VfM   31

Politics, society and economy: WWII (1939–1945) and its aftermath

WWII was a significant turning point in South African history, while the country was divided in terms of whether it should enter the war on the side of the Allies or whether it should support its neighbouring German communities – this was the first hurdle to overcome. South Africa eventually sided with the Allies and, in so doing, its soldiers of all ethnicities were brought into greater contact with the British and USA forces, where state intervention in these countries in relation to health and welfare was well entrenched. In 1944 the House of Assembly within South Africa requested the government to acknowledge its advice that there should be introduced "a comprehensive programme of legislation and administrative measures embracing the subjects of the provision of employment, social security, housing and public health, nutrition and education and that such a programme should constitute a people's charter".[80] These new provisions were also to be extended as it was found to enable a boost to the economic ability of the country. Smuts, Prime Minister at the time, was also planning to provide pensions, health and unemployment schemes akin to those found in Europe and extending original legislative provisions from 1937. This was most certainly the blueprint for a contribution-funded welfare state but was nonetheless controversial and by 1946 the Act excluded black mining workers and, before losing the election in 1948, rather than risk a white backlash, the welfare reforms as envisaged were pared back further.[81]

Black segregation policies increased in nature and after the general election in 1948, which Smuts lost, the white minority government imposed a formal policy of segregation. Apartheid sparked opposition from other African countries and international countries alike resulting in a significant embargos and sanctions being imposed in relation to arms, trade and sporting opportunities. Organisations including the United Nations, the International Olympic Committees, the World Health Organisations among others, all imposed different sanctions against apartheid rule. In spite of the global outcry against apartheid, South Africa continued its approach until 1990.

Politics, society and economy: 1960s–1972

The apartheid regime saw many protests within South Africa and among people in the UK, USA and other countries. Within this era, South Africa witnessed many riots, within which people either perished or were imprisoned as a result of the increasing protests against the apartheid system. The demonstrations saw many displaced and disaffected inhabitants from the townships march into Cape Town and Johannesburg and who continued their protests unrelentingly as support for the African Nationalist Congress (ANC) and Pan Africanist Congress (PAC) grew. Political activism grew in impetus as more and more countries sanctioned South Africa, in response to which the government utilised the Unlawful Organisations Act to ban the ANC and the PAC from any activity and a state of emergency was declared

32 The historic development of VfM

bringing in military force to control any demonstrations. Nelson Mandela was appointed as the President for the National Action Council confirming that this struggle was his life. Indeed, it was not only western countries that were imposing trading bans on South Africa, but also its neighbours, Ghana, Sierra Leone and Nigeria. This state of socioeconomic and political flux continued relentlessly throughout the 1960s and in 1962 Nelson Mandela was finally arrested and imprisoned, eventually tried and sentenced to life imprisonment in 1964, during the trial he again voiced that he would die fighting for democracy in South Africa if he had to.

Politics, society and economy: the influence of the EU 1972–2018

However, recession began to bite in the 1970s, as the UK was joining the EU, worldwide resistance to apartheid was increasing, foreign investment in South Africa and trade relations were decreasing. The inevitable impact on South Africa's economy was tangible, but the country continued to develop. The International Monetary Fund provided significant investment funds for South Africa during this period. As a result of which infrastructure developments progressed in what was, despite its unrest, a state developing into a capitalist economy. Other forms of investments were also being committed from private banking groups enabling the growth of the country. Infrastructure developments to upgrade and extend harbours, provide rail networks, electricity and energy supplies were being progressed, but by 1983 the public pressure on the IMF ensured that there was no further funding from that establishment. This withdrawal of financial assistance and investment stagnated the country's growth prospects, unemployment began to rise and the instability of the gold prices put further strain on the country.

By 1984 strike action was a recurring feature and township unrest increased. Once again military action was used to control the situation. Violent conflict ensued when 7,000 troops and policemen were drafted into the country. The instability of the country during this period meant that the private bank loans were called in leading the country further into recession. P.W. Botha had begun to have discussions with Nelson Mandela to discuss a peace settlement. The fall of the Berlin Wall and the continued massive pressure on apartheid by domestic and international forces meant that this system had to change and while F.W. De Clerk steered that change, Botha made the first inroads towards that peace process. Mandela was released in 1992 and by 1994 South Africa became a democracy under the presidency of Nelson Mandela and deputy presidency of F.W. De Clerk. From that point onward, South Africa gathered momentum as it began to roll back into becoming a global economy.

First, developing a just and fair constitution that recognised equality, a one-man-one–vote system, an administrative government and justice system akin to that of the UK. Flowing from such a constitution, which was finally proclaimed as an act of parliament in 1996, were the further

The historic development of VfM   33

advancements of government departments, to ensure that they operated in line with the new constitution and to curb historic corruption they were brought into line through the Public Finance Management Act of 1999. This act requires government departments to be auditable in their financial management of their functions. The legislation requires that departments are tracked to ensure that their financial management includes budgeting controls, accounting mechanisms, in conjunction with financial and performance information auditing with a clear aim of stamping out corruption, promoting effective planning for developments and advocating the need to achieve value for money, which is defined by Treasury Regulation 16 to the Public Finance Management Act 1999 to mean "the provision of the institutional function or the use of state property by a private party (in terms of a PPP project) to result in a net benefit to the institution defined in terms of cost, price, quality, risk transfer or a combination thereof". In addition to the steps being taken above it is also the case that since 2002 South Africa has subscribed to the UNCITRAL Model Law enacting its provisions for procurement onto its statute book to promote fairness in contracting, transparency and competitive processes to be undertaken to procure contractors working towards an efficient and effective procurement process.[82]

South Africa won the right to host the World Cup in 2010 and, in so doing, investment in transport networks increased to ensure that access was possible to each of the South African stadia to be used to facilitate the matches to be played. The World Cup put South Africa back on the world map in a positive and progressive light.

In its Annual Report from Treasury and its Minister of Finance in 2017, South Africa confirmed that one of its main quests was to tackle poverty and grow the economy and as a means to achieving that aim the report sets out within its development plan that it is to invest in a multibillion-rand development drive to "remedy the skewed implementation of infrastructure during the apartheid years" and to grasp the challenges of meeting the demands of a growing economy and an ever increasing population.

Johannesburg is now the largest city within South Africa, with a population of 7 million people;[83] it became established as a result of the gold and diamond mining industry. The inherent wealth flowing from those commodities ensured that the companies dealing within this market put their head office foundations at the heart of the city. The banking sector soon followed, which resulted in Johannesburg becoming the central financial hub for Africa. As a result of this growth, infrastructure development had taken place; however, it is stated that these developments were historically undertaken on an unregulated basis coupled with many other issues, including corruption and the theft of infrastructure once it has been installed. This has exacerbated the infrastructure problems faced not just in Johannesburg but in South Africa per se, covering everything from road works, electricity, drainage and water supplies.

34   *The historic development of VfM*

While it would be expected that unemployment in this area would be minimal, the opposite is, in fact, true. Unemployment is high, crime rates are high and poverty is endemic (ibid.). The rationale for this is that the "informal markets" have thrived above legitimate markets and therefore government suffers as a direct consequence. When it is impossible to estimate how many people are employed or not there is a distinct lack of ability to impose correct taxation levies and with a seeming lack of incentive for individuals to take up work the problem perpetuates. While a census has been carried out the dichotomy of the informal economy and the formal economy still needs to be addressed. Indeed, this informal market and extreme poverty underpin some of the reasons that infrastructure in Johannesburg is facing so many problems. Scrap metal being more of a beacon for the theft of the fabric of the infrastructure as its value is perceived to be more profitable for the men who steal it rather than any real value for the benefit of the economy or the future of the communities which such structures serve. Thus the mindset of the beneficiaries in this instance needs to be addressed, a VfM problem which to date has not been encountered within developed western continents.

While the matters raised above are being tackled, developments are ongoing. Housing schemes, cosmopolitan areas for shopping and a democratic, free market economy is growing, yet the townships still remain heavily populated.

India

Overview

India is a South Asian country, the seventh largest country in the world and the sixth biggest economy and reputed to be the fastest growing economy within the world currently (2018) with GDP in 2017 at $2.597 trillion.[84] It is surrounded by China, Bhutan, Nepal, Myanmar (Burma) Pakistan and Bangladesh. Geographically, India is a rich and diverse country featuring, mountain ranges, deserts, plateaux and coastal regions (ibid.). Not unlike Africa, its location and climate ensure that its economy is based on diverse commercial activities ranging from luxury spices, teas, coffees and raw materials. The economic activities within India have developed to include manufacturing and production with the fastest growing industry being that of IT. India has a strong sense of identity and has not throughout the years been without its own conflict and turmoil. Not unlike the other countries covered in this chapter, it has suffered at the expense of British invasion. However, there is also a high rate of poverty and a significant wealth and poverty gap reported. Infrastructure in some parts of India is woefully inadequate and corruption within public sector is not unknown. India's transition over the decades has been assisted by aid and relief funding from other countries, including the UK.

The historic development of VfM   35

Politics, society and economy: the early years

India in the 5th Century BC had developed political entities within the different states of the country they were established either as independent monarchies or tribal republics. This was an advanced society with developed cities around trading hubs. However, different warring factions that were seeking to expand their territories began to grow and develop into different complex empires. By the 1st Century AD, the Kushana Empire was one of the larger northern empires described as being "melting pots of culture". Even at this point in history India's trading opportunities were growing as the Roman Empire grew, the desire for the different goods and produce increased. The economic development began to gain impetus into the south of the country by the 2nd Century BC and the Tamil-speaking regions opened up trading ports. Trading routes and local networks of trade were being opened up across the different regions of India. Migration across the country was evident. Small settlements were appearing throughout the country. It appears that the country had three distinct empires and rulers who were all vying for imperial supremacy. The warring between the factions led to political and economic instability and, indeed, saw the three powers' strength weaken giving opportunity for a fourth faction, the Chola Empire, to challenge as a dominant force. The decline of Rome saw further development of trade links with Asia.[85]

India, having the benefit of being an important hub of international trade routes, connecting China to the Middle East even prior to 1500 AD, prospered under the Mughal Empire (1526–1748) in a period of time accredited to have being "Golden Age" for India. While under the rule of the Moghul Empire, Akbar (1556–1605) introduced a standardised taxation system, which advanced the feudal system that was operated prior to that (1206) established a form of government as a development from the early polities and monarchies and, in spite of religious unrest within India, his toleration policies ensured stability. Akbar had the political will to move into the south of India. The Moghul Empire held India for almost two centuries with policies of toleration, but by 1658, under the hands of Aurangzeb, the policies of toleration were being disaffected as a result of weaknesses in the economic structure of the country. It was also at this time that India was undergoing a sea-based invasion. The UK had firmly established itself on the shores of India and British supremacy within India was widely acknowledged by 1805 and Britain defended its supremacy vigorously and began to annexe its territories to expand its influence (ibid.).

South India was opposed to the British policies and colonialism seeing this invasion as a threat to the Indian way of life culminating in an uprising between north and central India, requiring the British crown to step in (1858) and take over the administration of India. As the British administration sought to model India on England, a new governance and civil service administration emerged.[86] The Indian National Congress was formed in 1855 taking an anti-imperialist stance and began seeking home rule. However,

36 *The historic development of VfM*

India was absorbed into the worldwide economy as a dependant of Britain and India's trade routes increased as the UK East India Company firmly established itself particularly as the Suez Canal opened. WWI distracted the position for a while, but after the war the British administration began to introduce repressive legislation and British intentions were brought into question, particularly as the trading routes increased trade to and from India during this period but by 1921 India was an under-developing country.

India at this time was also experiencing civil unrest over religious ideologies and a rise in riots took place between Hindu and Muslim believers.

The British influence on India was far reaching, culminating in the decision to partition India, thus creating the new country of Pakistan in 1947. The transition period saw bloody conflict as the religiously divided countries attempted to recreate themselves. However, from this period onwards India was thrown into almost continuous conflict. There have been three wars between India and Pakistan and one war between China and India, all with devastating consequences and significant loss of life. Such economic instability debilitated growth at this time.

Politics, society and economy: WWI (1914–1918) and its aftermath

India's involvement in WWI also sparked the initiative for independence from the UK. Almost 1.5 million Indian men volunteered in the Indian Expeditionary Force, in which it is held that 74,000 men lost their lives backing the UK. Economically, India also suffered as the war in Europe required supplies and basic commodities that were exported from India in vast quantities, leaving India with scarce resources for its own needs. Prices rose sharply and UK subsidies were diverted from India to the UK to finance the war. India did, however, increase its production of linen as the cotton mills of Lancashire declined. Steel could now also be exported as the Tata Steel Mills was awarded the contract to produce the materials for the development of the railway lines for the transportation of troops. Within India, the political forces were once again becoming hostile to British imperialism and by 1920 this has escalated to a position of non-cooperation.

Politics, society and economy: WWII (1939–1945) and its aftermath

Economically, India was not benefiting and unrest continued until 1935 when the British conceded full autonomy to India through the Government of India Act, but, in spite of this, India did not achieve full independence until 1947. Even after this time turmoil prevailed for many different reasons, including religion and famine. As with WWI, the demand for food to feed the troops was to be met by Asia, causing a rise in food prices to the population of India while traders stockpiled food to sell overseas. The result was the Bengal famine in 1943, which is held to have been linked to over 2 million deaths, since estimated to be nearer to 4 million. The exit of the British from India after partition left two countries, India and Pakistan, in turmoil and constant conflict. The political impetus was to build those nations but religious altercations continued.

India's economic growth was also stagnated by the fact that the opposing political factions were either closely linked to the business elite and capitalist systems, which believed that minimal state intervention was the best policy, or the socialist movements. The first Prime Minister, Nehru, had a socialist background, who opted to govern on the basis of a centrally planned economy as a form of compromise between communism, on the one hand, and capitalism, on the other. He also determined that he would not align India to either of the global powers at that time. This is seen to have been a good strategic decision as during the Cold War India was able to rely on aid from all. It is, however, stated that India has itself created a position of endemic poverty from a systematic failure to eliminate basic deprivations and impose adequate state interventions in the areas of education, health and welfare care; instead India introduced its first five-year plan in 1951, which began to centralise the economy and nationalise its industries. This move of self-reliance and closed economy stagnated the economic development of India even further. Nehru was criticized for being over–bureaucratic, which inhibited competition, innovation, efficiency and economic growth, a recurring theme throughout each country to achieving a good basis of governance. This is one of the first times within early Indian history that any reference is made to reforms to promote efficiency and competition.

Politics, society and economy: 1960s–1972

The Green Revolution in India in 1960 came about to address the food shortages that India was blighted by.[87] The revolution saw the introduction of modern technologies and methods of farming that assisted India in its journey to self-sufficiency, but it worked on its principles of protectionism and economic interventionism, with a large government and business regulation with policies akin to those of the Soviet Union set out within the five-year plans. The biggest success factor in this period was the introduction of high yield varieties of different seeds such as wheat and this went some way to addressing issues of famine and low food production in areas that were prone to drought.

Politics, society and economy: the influence of the EU 1972–2018

India suffered economically again in 1991, needing to borrow significantly from the IMF and the World Bank. In borrowing from these organisations and, indeed, as a result of India's economic position, it was compelled to review its trading policies. It reduced its tariffs for imports and capital allowing other countries to participate in what had previously been an inaccessible market. It was not until the Ministry of Finance opened up the

38 *The historic development of VfM*

economy in this way that India has started to grow as a major economic competitor within the worldwide market.

It is being said that the success of the changes to a free market has given rise to a "sizeable middle class" yet poverty and deprivation remain endemic. This significant wealth gap needs to be addressed across each of the 26 states. The new "globalisation" policy being adopted by India, which is promoting the need to attract investment, is using that form of carrot within each of its states to ensure that they seek to grow and develop in line with the aim of India in becoming a world superpower, an accolade it is quickly achieving.

India has also understood that, in order for it to continue to develop and grow within this market, its infrastructure needs to be developed to accommodate this position and it is undertaking a number of PPP initiatives to forge its developments forward, India's policy on public–private partnerships being that they work together in harmony. However, it is stated that its processes and procedures are fragmented and that the rules have not supported the desired results. The criticism is that there are a number of general financial rules and procurement manuals but there is no legislative backing to give significance to this system.[88] Indeed, its legislative framework is nothing more than a "motley set of guidelines". India, however, in terms of its recourse to public procurement has acceded to comply with the provisions of UNCITRAL Model Law, albeit that this does appear to be limited to the procurement elements only while other aspects are being debated. The acceptance of this model will obviously require transparent processes to be implemented, which evidentially we can state creates VfM or a public value approach.

Conclusion

What is evident from all that we have seen within each of the stages of the countries as they have developed is that one country can have a dramatic impact on another in a worldwide environment. Historically, this impact has seen both negative and positive effects, some negative effects debilitating countries for centuries and positive effects lifting countries out of economic and political despair. The different journeys that each of these countries has made in its development on the worldwide stage are significant, but evidence highlights that each of the countries has undergone internal conflict, political instability, wars, financial instability, a need to rely on external financial assistance and disasters, some natural, some man made, some economical and others environmental; and at each juncture each one has moved on and progressed. The different stages within this progression can be clearly identified and while it appears that the UK in its discussions and debates about value for money are slightly more advanced than those of the others, that can perhaps be linked to the cycle of development and the stages of development of each. The recurring theme across each of the countries as it advances into market economies and developed nations is that there is a need to promote efficiency, effectiveness and economy in its dealings, whether that is in the realms of public sector procurements or, indeed, whether there are private dealings.

However, in spite of the different historic socioeconomic, political and cultural differences between each, the need to achieve the concept of value for money as a socioeconomic and political drive can be seen in each to be based on either a threat or a promise. The threat being that if you do not achieve it somehow, you have lost and must be penalised; but if you do achieve it or you can provide it, you win. The dichotomy here is that no one knows whether they are winning or losing as achieving value for money while appearing to be borne of a need to combat corruption, drive efficiency and effectiveness and improve competition, it is neither sufficiently defined to enable a measurable or auditable result to be confirmed nor is there a tangible mechanism by which to measure or track the success or failure of the plight.

Notes

1 (Public Accounts Committee (UK), 2007)
2 (Public Accounts Committee (UK), 2007)
3 (BBC History, 2018)
4 (Heller, 2003)
5 (Historical Association, 2015)
6 (Public Accounts Committee (UK), 2007)
7 (Public Accounts Committee (UK), 2007)
8 Ibid.
9 Ibid.
10 Ibid.
11 (Chantril, 2018)
12 (Historical Association, 2015)
13 (Public Accounts Committee (UK), 2007)
14 (Talbot, 2010)
15 (Overy, 2011)
16 (BBC History, 2018)
17 (Fairhurst, 2007)
18 (Chantril, 2018)
19 (BBC History, 2018)
20 (BBC History, 2018)
21 (Chantril, 2018)
22 (Overy, 2011)
23 (Heller, 2003)
24 (BBC History, 2018)
25 (Overy, 2011)
26 (Public Accounts Committee (UK), 2007)
27 (Public Accounts Committee (UK), 2007)
28 (BBC History, 2018)
29 (The Historical Association, 2015)
30 (Talbot, 2010)
31 (BBC History, 2018)
32 (Chantril, 2018)

40   *The historic development of VfM*

33 (Chantril, 2018)
34 (Public Accounts Committee (UK), 2007)
35 (Fairhurst, 2007)
36 (Bennett & Cirrell, 2009)
37 (BBC History, 2018)
38 (Office for National Statistics, 2018)
39 (Chantril, 2018)
40 (Marshall, 2016)
41 (Overy, 2011)
42 (Marshall, 2016)
43 (Australian National University, 2018)
44 (Kun, 2014)
45 (Overy, 2011)
46 (Kun, 2014)
47 (Marshall, 2016)
48 (Kun, 2014)
49 (Australian National University, 2018)
50 (History.com, 2017)
51 (Overy, 2011)
52 (Overy, 2011)
53 (History.com, 2017)
54 (Overy, 2011)
55 (Encyclopaedia Britannica, 2018)
56 (BBC History, 2018)
57 (Overy, 2011)
58 (Mulhahan, 2019)
59 (Encyclopaedia Britannica, 2018)
60 (Encyclopaedia Britannica, 2018)
61 (History.com, 2017)
62 (Gong, 2009)
63 (Overy, 2011)
64 (Australian Bureau of Statistics, n.d.)
65 (Aboriginal Heritage Office, 2017)
66 (Overy, 2011)
67 (Aboriginal Heritage Office, 2017)
68 (Aboriginal Heritage Office, 2017)
69 (Overy, 2011)
70 (Australian Government, 2017)
71 (O'Flynne, 2007)
72 (Australian National University, 2018)
73 (Marshall, 2016)
74 (Overy, 2011)
75 (Overy, 2011)
76 (BBC History, 2018)
77 (Overy, 2011)
78 (South African Government, 2018)
79 (BBC History, 2018)
80 (Stapelton, 2016)
81 (BBC History, 2018)
82 (South African Government, 2018)
83 (BBC History, 2018)
84 (Marshall, 2016)
85 (Overy, 2011)
86 (Cultural India.Net, 2017)

87 (Living History Farm, 2016)
88 (Jena & Hazarika, 2017)

Works cited

Aboriginal Heritage Office. (2017). *A Brief Aboriginal History*. Retrieved from www.aboriginalheritage.org/history

Arrowsmith, S. (1996). *The Law of Public Utilities and Procurement*. Oxford: Sweet & Maxwell.

Australian Bureau of Statistics. (n.d.). *Population*. Retrieved from www.abs.gov.au/population

Australian Government. (2017). *How Government Works*. Retrieved from www.australia.gov.au/about-government

Australian National University. (2018). *Value for Money: Budget and Financial Management Reform om the People's Republic of China, Taiwan and Australia* (A. Podger, T.-T. Su, J. Wanna, H.-S. Chan, & N. Meili, Eds.). Canberra: Australian National University.

BBC History. (2018). Retrieved from http://www.bbc.co.uk/history/british/pm_and_pol_tl_01.shtml

Bennett, J. & Cirrell, S. (2009). *EC Public Procurement Law and Practice Manual*. Oxford: Sweet & Maxwell.

Byrne, T. (2000). *Local Government in Britain*. London: Penguin.

Chantril, C. (2018). *Charts of Past Spening*. Retrieved from https://www.ukpublicspending.co.uk/past_spending

Cultural India.Net. (2017). *History of India: Facts, Timelines, Personalities and Culture*. Retrieved from https://www.culturalindia.net/indian-history/index.html

Encyclopaedia Britannica. (2018, 13 April). Retrieved from https://www.britannica.com/place/United-Kingdom/Society-state-and-economy

Fairhurst, J. (2007). *The Law of the European Union* (6th ed.). London: Pearson.

Gong, T. (2009). Institutional Learning and Adaptation: Developing State Audit in China. *Public Administration and Development*, 33–41.

Heller, M. (2003). *London Clerical Workers 1880–1914: The Search for Stability*. London: University College London.

Her Majesty's Treasury (HMT). (2006). *Value for Money Asssessment Guidance*. London: HMSO.

Historical Association. (2015). *History. Org.UK*. Retrieved from https://www.history.org.uk/primary/resource/3859/britain-since-1930-a-brief-history

History.com. (2017, December). *The Early Chinese Empires*. Retrieved from www.history.com/topics/ancient-china

Hutton, W. (1995). *The State We Are In*. London: Vintage.

Jena, P.R. & Hazarika, B. (2017). *Public Procurement in India: Assessment of Institutional Mechanism, Challenges and Reforms*. New Delhi: National Institute of Public Finance Policy.

Kun, Z. (2014, May). *Critical Issues in the Next Decade of China's Infrastructure Effort*. Retrieved 22 August 2018

Living History Farm. (2016). Retrieved from India and Pakistan Farming in the 1950s and 1960s https://livinghistoryfarm.org/farminginthe50s/crops_16.html

Marshall, T. (2016). *Prisoners of Geography*. London: Elliott & Thompson.

Mulhahan, K. (2019). *Making China Modern*. Harvard, CA: Harvard University Press.

42 *The historic development of VfM*

National College for Teaching and Leadership. (2016). *Improving Efficiency and Strategic Management*. Retrieved from https://www.nationalcollege.org.uk/transfer/open/dsbm-phase-4-module-3-improving-efficiency-and-strategic-management/historical-perspective/dsbm-p4m3-s2t1.html

Office for National Statistics. (2018, January). *People,Population and Community*. Retrieved from www.ons.gov,uk/people/populationandcommunity

O'Flynne, J. (2007). From New Public Management to Public Value: Paradigmatic Change and Managerial Implications. *Australian Journal of Public Administration*, 353–366.

Overy, R. (2011). *The Times Complete History of the World* (8th ed.). London: Time Books London.

Public Accounts Committee (UK). (2007). *Holding Government to Account: 150 Years of the Committee of Public Accounts 1857–2007*. London: HMT.

South African Government. (2018). *History/ South Africa Government*. Retrieved from www.gov.za/about-za

Stapelton, T. (2016). *Union of South Africa*. International Encyclopedia of the First World War.

Talbot, C. (2010). *Performance in Government: The Evolving System of Performance and Evaluation Measurement, Monitoring and Management in the United Kingdom*. Washington, DC: Independent Evaluation Group of the World Bank.

2 Tracking VfM: concept, definition, benchmark, tracking and testing

The VfM concept

A concept is something viewed in the abstract or something that is formulated as a general idea or principle, the beginning or starting point for something to be tested such as a prototype.[1] VfM is a concept and arguably can only ever be conceptual because of its subjectivity and its need to change to accommodate the demands of distinctly different projects, different time factors and different stakeholder needs. Unhelpfully, the concept and often the projects to which it is associated have a mercurial character, changing on a temporal basis as societal, political, legal or stakeholder requirements and needs change. These changes cannot always be fixed in time, changes continue as projects develop, unexpected events happen and project risks pass from one stakeholder to another.

The very nature of a subjective concept is that it is also capable of interpretation by anyone, in any way, to align with personal perceptions, the premise that "beauty is in the eye of the beholder" or the idea that "all that glitters is not gold" are just two often used expressions, but these merely simply scratch the surface of the problems associated with trying to achieve a one-size-fits-all definition. In order to attempt to formulate a workable solution that can be tracked, tested and confirmed, there are numerous elements that must be captured. Rutherford has defined some of the subjective influences of VfM with the acronym SLEEPT, the social, legal, economic, environmental, political and technical elements of VfM.[2] This particular analysis, while sufficiently wide in a generic way to encapsulate all aspect of qualitative and quantitative measures, is *too* generic, thereby missing nuances such as the aims, expectations and outputs to be achieved by the project.

In the UK, we saw that the need to require the achievement of VfM when purchasing by the public sector was initially used as a tool to measure a reasonable price. This foundation grew into the need to "make inquiry into the receipt, issue and audit of public money" as stated by the Public Accounts Committee (PAC) in the UK, and then as a mechanism to "curb improper spending and wasting of public money". Progressing into "looking beyond the formality of the expenditure but also to its wisdom, faithfulness and economy". In all of the statements made by the PAC, the concept has developed based on a

44 *Tracking VfM*

need to address a negative action, but there is no clarity or direction set out to encapsulate how the achievement of that VfM goal should be undertaken, with the exception of the later arrival of the UK Treasury's guidance relating to ex ante and ex post reviews, which are fundamentally inadequate.

This position also seems to be reflected in the practices undertaken by Australia, China, India and Africa; as each nation develops economically, its VfM requirements and expectations shift to address socioeconomic, legal and political agenda, as highlighted in Figure 2.1.

In China, it is seen that expectations have shifted from those linked to state-controlled commune-based economies, in which the state controlled everything for everyone, including prices for available goods and services, where quality and quantity would not be questioned, to a free market economy. The transition giving rise to the need to implement effective mechanisms to "control extravagant position related consumerism" and more recently to promote "effectiveness, cost control and efficiency".[3] In 2004 the UK Treasury prepared a report for the Chinese government in relation to the achievement of VfM in procurement of public–private partnerships, which was very much based on the very early guidance used by the UK, one startling point being that the UK did not share its up-to-date (2004) thinking to address the needs of China, rather it took two steps back to the simple use of the Public Sector Comparator test, it did not share the look-forward and look-back test review provisions. Indeed, it can be seen that the legislative parameters contained within the UNCITRAL Model Law (2011) as adopted by China, governing the procurement processes, do not seem to advocate the need to achieve VfM. The tendering requirements simply state that procurements are assessed on lowest price evaluation, or a comprehensive assessment, in which the overriding principles are to promote openness, transparency, fair competition, impartiality and honesty. The requirement to achieve VfM is not a primary consideration. This is arguably because of the state of the nation in terms of the overriding need to drive out corruption in dealings.

South Africa seems only recently to be realising the need to address the point to combat corruption and to address more social issues, which are linked to a prevailing informal economy, inevitably undermining the real economy, particularly highlighted in Johannesburg, and to address the inequalities of the apartheid years. The South African government has therefore taken the first step and incorporated the concept of achieving value for money within the South African Constitution as a defined term.[4] This is further underpinned within the Public Finance Management Act (1999), which sets out that the procuring public department must ensure an appropriate procurement and provisioning system. The system must be based on the principles of being fair, equitable, transparent, competitive and cost effective replicating the UNCITRAL doctrine, but with the main focus of the principles being heavily weighted to transparency of dealings and ensuring a competitive arena, to address the prevailing social problems. Creation of employment, driving out corruption within procurement and eradicating

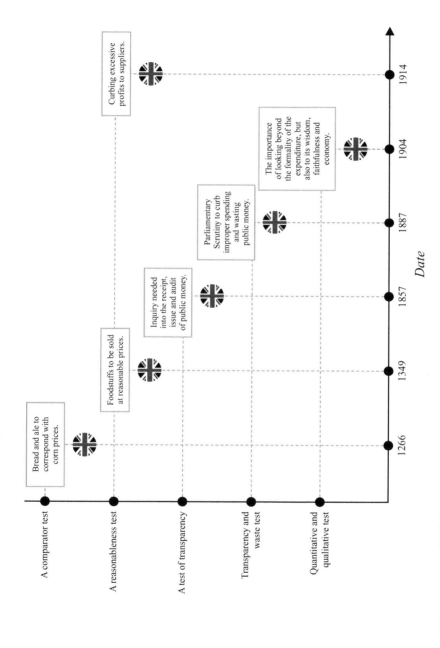

Figure 2.1 A timeline of VfM tests
Source: Kalluk and Neonakis (2018, pp. 23–24)

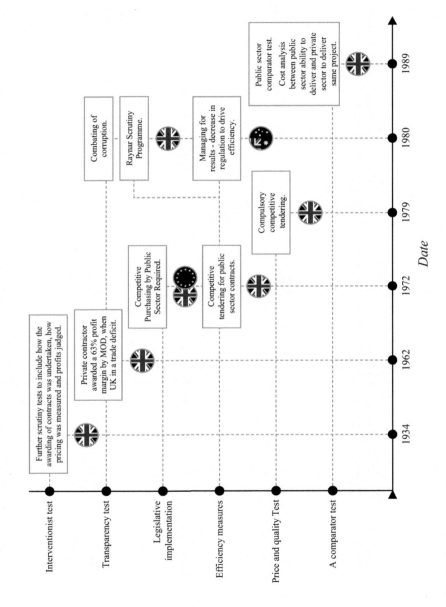

Figure 2.1 (Cont.)

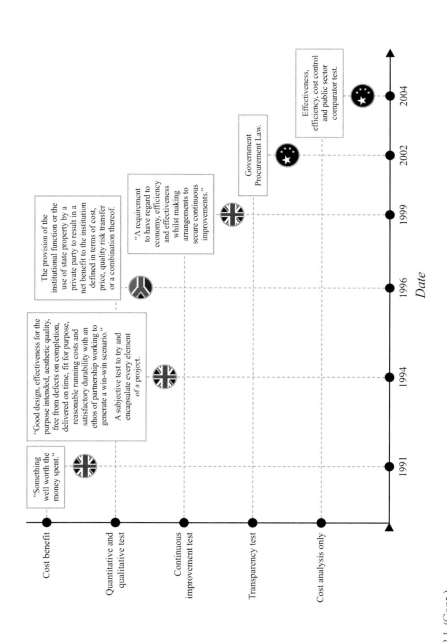

Figure 2.1 (Cont.)

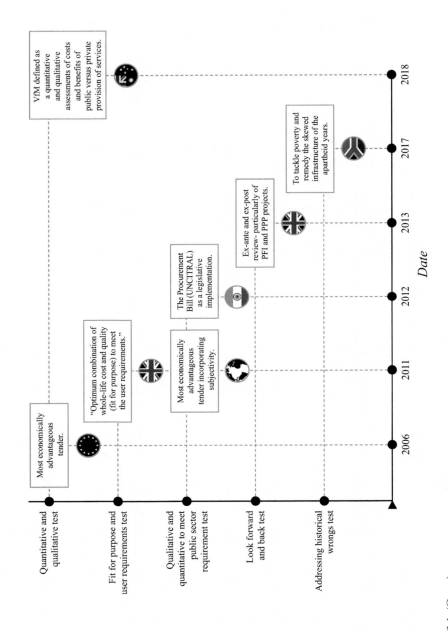

Figure 2.1 (Cont.)

historical discriminations being the overriding aims of the South African procurement strategies.

The rise in public awareness of corruption in South Africa has resulted in the establishment of the National Anti-Corruption hotline and other such initiatives to try and address the problem. The tendering process undertaken by the public authorities in South Africa is based on a method of assessing tenders based on a preferential points system, which prescribes functionality, price and other categories of concern such as "ensuring that contracting is with persons or categories of persons historically disadvantaged."[5] This all underpins the message that VfM is, in fact, a consequence arising out of addressing other matters.

The position in India is rather different, because, while India has myriad guidelines expressing how to undertake procurements, there are no national legislative provisions to entrench the procedures. The General Financial Rules 2005 contained broad guidelines for procurement with a focus on transparency and integrity and, following on from India's decision to adopt the United Nation's Commission on International Trade Law (UNCITRAL) Model Law in 2012, there was the publication of the Public Procurement Bill in that same year, which advocated the UN principles to ensure transparency, accountability and probity, ensure fair and equitable treatment, promote competition, enhance efficiency and economy and maintain integrity and public confidence in procurement, but the Public Procurement Bill's journey into legislation has been a prolonged process and, once again, the achievement of VfM is not obligatory.

Prior to the adoption of the UNCITRAL model, as a key governance mechanism, the Supreme Court of India underpinned further the need to ensure probity in processes and in a telecommunications case coming before it, arrived at a decision relating to procurement behaviours, to strike down contracts awarded where it had been shown that the contract allowed for significant profit and windfall gains to the private sector and/or where fraud and corruption were evident. Again, it is the case that VfM, while being mooted as important, does not focus as a primary concern, rather the important socioeconomic interests are the dominant feature.

In view of all of the above, it is apparent that the legislative parameters and other tests that have been implemented, from comparison tests through reasonableness and transparency to interventionist tests, were all initially set out to achieve the curbing of corruption or efficacy of spending, not to achieve a VfM utopia. Therefore, major debates continue in the pursuance of a one-size-fits-all definition. On that basis, the chapter continues to review how the concept has journeyed into the legislative arena.

Definitions, tests and the legislative arena of VfM

While we have learned that in order to define VfM there are insurmountable hurdles to overcome, it remains the position, however, that there is a need to formulate some mechanism to benchmark how VfM is understood

50 *Tracking VfM*

and tested. Unless such a mechanism is achieved, ultimately the debates are futile, as VfM will always be a concept that cannot be properly tested.

The Organisation for Economic Cooperation and Development (OECD) has called for a sensible debate to achieve a VfM definition and more recently, in September 2018, the Construction Industry Council began an initiative with UK central government to work on a mechanism to track the process and develop the software to achieve it.

The starting point, however, must be to review the definitions, tests and legislative parameters that have developed over time within each of the countries, to provide an understanding or a baseline definition as a precursor to establishing a tracking and testing mechanism. Quite significantly, it can be seen that price or cost considerations override qualitative elements in the early years in every country.

Not dissimilar to the concept, the definitions have also been drafted historically to give flexibility. While this means that the definitions can be used across myriad infrastructure projects, the absence of hard rules or clarity of requirements leaves uncertainty. While parliamentary scrutiny and guidelines are prevalent from 1266 in the UK, it was not until the 1970s that the first legislation was introduced, but it remained that the achievement of VfM was not the primary aim of the legislation. The main aim, it appears, of that first legislation was simply to ensure that a competitive procurement process was entrenched within public sector purchasing.

VfM in its own right gained momentum in the early 1980s in the UK. In order to progress the modernisation of infrastructure, the UK government introduced the Private Finance Initiative (PFI), a contracting model that allowed private sector contractors to finance infrastructure projects, such as hospitals and schools, among others, by using financing deals obtained from private sector finance companies. The rationale for this initiative is a subject in its own right and out of the scope of this book; however, as a result of this new PFI process, before a contracting authority could enter into contract with a contractor for the significant sums associated with such projects, the contracting authority must have proved to the UK Treasury that the project was VfM. On that basis, in 1982, Sir William Ryrie generated the "Ryrie Rules" as the mechanism to test the VfM point of a PFI project. While this was developed to test PFI projects initially, it has since that time been used to test non-PFI infrastructure and other projects. This founding assessment was based on a purely quantitative test known as a Private Sector Comparator (PSC) test, which had as its methodology the requirement to show that the use of the PFI, when benchmarked against an equivalent private sector project, would result in a more "cost effective project than a publicly funded project", which was based on the premise that "projects must yield benefits in the form of improved efficiencies and profit, commensurate with the cost of raising risk capital", giving the impression that the risk in the project must be commensurate with the risk of the finance.

The Ryrie Rules, however, were deemed to be impossible benchmarks to achieve and in 1989 John Major, in his capacity of Chief Secretary to the Treasury, relaxed the rules in a two-stage process in 1989 and 1992 explaining that:

> [I]n 1989, the requirement of the public sector comparator was to be dropped **when** the private sector takes full responsibility for the success or failure of a project, and in 1992, the need for the comparator was to be dropped **if** the private sector is wholly responsible for a government project which needs government approval and can recoup all of its costs at the point of use, or where public finance would not be considered affordable in the foreseeable future.

The use of the words "when" and "if" (here emboldened for ease of reference) highlight that the ability to drop the PSC can only happen when the given circumstances exist. The wording above also suggests that some PFI projects could be considered outside this provision, as the private sector does not necessarily take full responsibility for the success or failure of a project.

PFI and later PF2 are or were synonymous with the position that who is best able to manage the risk also bears the responsibility and this premise seems to be a sensible approach, as it also lends weight to the notion that, while VfM is only judged at this time from the public sector perspective, in reality, it should be considered from all perspectives as risk is managed within projects by different stakeholders at different times. This principle can be applied to any form of infrastructure project or PPP being undertaken either by the public sector or, indeed, a private sector development project. The problem arises when trying to measure or compare innovate projects that do not have a comparator and this is a problem that the use of the PSC faces and a problem that the People's Republic of China will have faced when deciding to undertake the development of the innovative known as the Three Gorges Dam. The PSC therefore remains in situ, but to be used where it is possible as part of a quantitative and qualitative analysis.

It is also the case that, in 1989, legislation was enacted in the UK that codified the requirement for a public sector entity to achieve best value through its contracting practices. It is notable that the legislation introduces best value as a duty and not value for money. This position arose in response to the Conservative government's privatisation policy at the time; compulsory competitive tendering having been imposed on public sector entities through government guidance was not being followed effectively and therefore statutory provisions were required to ensure that government missives were being adhered to.

Again, it is notable that significant elements of a real VfM test were omitted not only from the Ryrie Rules, but also from the best value legislation and thus the ability to measure economically the subjective elements or ultimate outputs from a project at this stage were bypassed.

The Byatt Report in 1986 examined how to measure or apply "an appropriate measure of economic cost" to things that did not have a tangible

52 Tracking VfM

worth, as this report pre-dated the best value legislation, it is arguable that the wider application of the VfM concept across public sector purchasing was not being considered; if it were then surely it would have been included in the drafting of the 1989 legislation. However, the Byatt Report was developed to determine initially how to value nationalised industries and to give guidance about how such industries ought to be reporting their worth. This report or further advancements to it ought well to be utilised in terms of assessing how VfM should be considered; public sector buildings, hospitals, schools and other infrastructure projects have a social worth for a prolonged period of time, which could well be quantified at key dates or milestones. It is a little naive to omit this worth out of the equation as, ultimately, from a public sector perspective the performance of the project and the outputs generated therefrom are the real reason for undertaking the development in the first instance.

It is therefore appropriate to consider the principles arising from the Byatt Report when trying to establish a framework or mechanism to value public sector capital assets and services, which are not as a matter of course dealt with in the realms of a market economy. The report identifies issues such as accounting for economic costs and changing prices along with the problems related to the lack of "available market valuations allowing for a current value of either equity or net worth, which may have served as a denominator in a calculation for a rate of return based on current values" (Byatt). Nowhere in the report does it say that such things cannot be measured. Indeed, it is recognised by the Construction Research and Innovation Strategy Panel (CRiSP), and the Department for Business Innovation and Skills in the UK that additionality in development and regeneration interventions has a worth and a VfM impact. The research being undertaken by CRiSP in this area, while it does not deal directly with VfM, highlights the economic benefits to society and communities, where such redevelopment projects take place and investigates the returns for the communities that are generated therefrom. Arguably this should form part of the wider VfM debate as invariably, and unfortunately more often than not, public and political critics of projects use the emotional elements of a project to highlight its lack of VfM rather than the actual measure. The UK National Infrastructure Plan (2014) also identifies the benefits to economic growth for communities and stability derived from such interventions.

The 1986 Byatt Report also held that non-commercialised activities are not always sufficiently clear in definition to enable a valuation. However, it is arguable that the majority of non-commercial activities that are identified as part of a local authority's corporate strategy and the stakeholder's business cases and subsequent feasibility reports can be valued. If it is not possible to place a monetary value or measurement against non-commercialised benefits, they should nevertheless still not be ignored. On that basis, it is arguable that all elements should form part of the VfM assessment as it is possible that a stakeholder group member can derive a benefit at each stage of the procurement process, given that, at each stage, there is an expectation to be achieved.

While this is supported by the European Investment Bank's European PPP Expertise Centre (EPEC), there is a failure to take into account the benefits that are achieved by all stakeholder groups. This is evidenced both by the definitions provided for the concept and the way in which VfM is analysed through the UK Treasury Green Book provisions and as the other countries are either being advised by the UK or are following its lead, we can assume that the same position applies.

It was also the case that not all cost considerations were taken into account within the procurement of infrastructure projects; one distinct gap is that the actual cost of borrowing did not form part of the VfM consideration, particularly in relation to PFI, this was the subject of much criticism within parliament and parliamentary committees and showed a distinct lack of both transparency and highlighted bad financial management by Treasury in this area.

As part of the public sector process for identifying VfM, options appraisals should be undertaken, as such options appraisals not only provide information about the cost of the proposed project but they look at all the possible options available to each stakeholder to ultimately inform it of whether it should undertake a project or indeed determine what route the project should take; the information gathered in following such a process also informs negotiation positions for each of the stakeholders. The Byatt Report (1986) stated that:

> [T]he emphasis which is put on the bottom line figure (being the lowest negotiation parameter), whilst as a measure is undoubtedly important it should only be the start of the appraisal and not the conclusion.

The bottom line figure for each project should then be used as a benchmark against which other options can be tested, as the lowest cost does not necessarily achieve a VfM solution. The VfM testing provisions set out that, in order to undertake a VfM assessment, the base case or bottom line position must be established and further options appraisals should be undertaken to determine all available solutions. While this is an obligation to be undertaken in terms of the development of appropriate business plans, Hodge portrays this process as a fudge, an area of assessment that can be susceptible to manipulation and clever accounting. While it could be stated that clever accounting can manipulate any circumstance, the Green Book provisions require the financial assessments to take account of a number of different biases and project sensitivities to attempt to ensure that all possible economic, financial, project and accounting biases and risks are factors to be considered in advance.

It is not until the Latham Report in 1994 that quality and fitness for purpose are addressed, thus giving the foundation for the definition to include such elements. This qualitative element, however, is not considered again until the HMT definition in 2011 and even then, it can be seen, by the fact that this element is bracketed within the definition, that the implication is that this was either an afterthought in the drafting, or perhaps to be retained as an option going forward.

54 *Tracking VfM*

In pursuing the need to achieve a definition it is arguable that one could look to the definition emitting from the European Commission, of the Most Economically Advantageous Tender (MEAT), provisions as set out within the Public Contracts Regulations 2006 at r. 30 (as amended within the Public Contracts Regulations 2015 (PCR 2015)), which is advocated by the European parliament (2014) as a mechanism to ensure that value for money is achieved. This definition is now set out in the 2015 Regulations at r. 67 and is advocated to be implemented based on the perspective of the contracting authority as follows:

PCR 2015 sets out "that the tender shall be identified on the basis of the price or cost, using a cost-effectiveness approach, such as life-cycle costing, and may include the best price quality ration, which shall be assessed on the basis of criteria, such as qualitative, environmental and /or social aspects, linked to the subject-matter of the public contract in question"

Such criteria may include, for example:

- Quality, including technical merit, aesthetic and functional characteristics, accessibility, design for all users, social, environmental and innovative characteristics, trading and its conditions;
- Organisation, qualification and experience of staff assigned to performing the contract, where the quality of the staff assigned can have a significant impact on the level of the performance of the contract; or
- After-sales service and technical assistance, delivery conditions such as delivery date, delivery process and delivery period or period of completion;
- The cost element may also take the form of a fixed price or cost on the basis of which economic operators will compete on quality criteria only.

This, in effect, provides a tick list of elements that any contracting authority has the discretion to use, based on the subject matter of the project to be undertaken and indeed the socioeconomic need being addressed.

It is also possible to compare the above European standard to that of the standard set out in (UNCITRAL), which is the Model Law devised in (2011) to be adapted by international trading nations to provide a level playing field among the countries subscribing to use the template and (UNCITRAL) guidance. The Model Law is drafted to be applicable across many nations and, again, interestingly provides at Article 9 (2) that "suppliers or contractors shall meet such of the following criteria as procuring entity considers appropriate and relevant in the circumstances of the particular procurement"; However, Article 8 attempts to establish that the description of the goods, works, services or the goods to be the subject matter of the procurement must be described objectively and functionally, which seems to establish that there is no room for "subjectivity"; this seems to be supported within the terms set out for the evaluation criteria within Article 11:

(1 … the evaluation criteria shall relate to the subject matter of the procurement; and

(2 The evaluation criteria relating to the subject matter of the procurement may include:

- Price; and
- The cost of operating, maintaining and repairing goods or of construction; the time for delivery of goods, completion of construction or provision of services; the characteristics of the subject matter of the procurement, such as the functional characteristics of goods or construction and the environmental characteristics of the subject matter; and the terms of payment and of guarantees in respect of the subject matter of the procurement

(3 in addition to the criteria set out in Article 11 (2) as above, the evaluation criteria may include:

- Any criteria that the procurement regulations or other provisions of law of the State implementing the Model Law, authorises or requires to be taken into account; and
- A margin of preference for the benefit of the domestic suppliers or contractors or for domestically produced goods, or any other preference, if authorised or required by the procurement regulations or other provisions of law of the State.

Interestingly, the PCR 2015 regulations put more emphasis on quality, social and innovation factors over price analysis alone than the UNCITRAL Model Law does, which has more of a focus on the objective elements of functionality, deliverability and environmental elements. Aesthetic characteristics are not even a feature, unless they are contained within state-specific requirements and, as we have evidenced above, the sample of countries using the Model Law provisions are only doing so to address the socioeconomic problems that affect the individual country and impact on the ability to trade across borders effectively and competitively. The aesthetics of a project do not even warrant a mention within the debate of those countries as yet.

The predominant feature within (UNCITRAL) is the requirement for transparency within all dealings, indicative of the need to address the reputation that developing countries have in combatting elements of corruption in procurement processes. Corruption has a significant negative impact on the ability to achieve VfM. Thus, the functionality of the Model Law focuses on achieving VfM by ensuring on all levels that the stakeholders are being treated transparently, rather than trying to ensure that an appropriate "subjective" tender based on quality alone is dealt with. Arguably, this reflects the differences in needs as between an advanced market economy found within many westernised countries, when compared to emerging and developing countries, and where they are in terms of socio-political and legal development, not simply the economic positioning of the country. If it were

56 Tracking VfM

based purely on the economic position of the country then India and China ought well to be more advanced in this process than the UK.

Looking at the analysis of each of the definitions that have been used over time, either through legislative imposition or by concepts arising from finance departments, or the European Union, and any other country legislative provisions, it can mostly be seen that each definition or concept permits the achievement of both objective and subjective elements, but even with a definition as a tick list of options, not dissimilar to the EU's MEAT provision or the UNCITRAL definition, every element of subjectivity is not going to be included or even achievable.

A potential remedy to this problem would be to utilise the MEAT definition. The rationale for this is that MEAT is determined on a project-by-project basis and it is not necessarily restricted to infrastructure projects alone, as the PCR are intended to cover every possible procurement. The definition emitting from the MEAT concept can also be utilised by each of the stakeholder groups, to any project process, when each stakeholder is at the inception of a project or undertaking its own due diligence in order to determine whether it participates in the project or not, each stakeholder can identify what its aims and objectives are for becoming involved in a particular project using the MEAT criterion as a benchmark. This can be seen from a pragmatic application of the theory in Chapter 5. Irrespective of the assertion within the regulations that it is to be used from a public sector-specific assessment, each stakeholder should be able to use the tick list for its own project needs and the order of priority for each element or measure of VfM that can be agreed at the pre-tender stage, it may well be that the order of priority is different for each stakeholder at each juncture, but in order to achieve each of the stakeholder's project aims, the priority is based on individual circumstances and is not a collective decision. The expectations can then be captured within the contractual drafting and used to form the foundation of a process for achieving VfM on a project-specific basis. This process can then be tracked on an ongoing basis by a simple tracking system, for the benefit of all stakeholder groups. Thus moving away from trying to find a "one-size-fits-all" definition would accord with the MEAT process, and would direct debate away from trying to find a "precise measurement that does not exist". In spite of the existence of the HMT definition and the Green Book mechanisms, HMT frameworks and guidance, 242 of them in total dating back to the early 1970s, there is still a strong reliance on cost–benefit analysis and despite a shift by Treasury towards incorporating ex post and ex ante reviews, this process has still not found its way through to public sector infrastructure practices predominantly because very few modern-day projects have reached their optimal conclusions. As a result, it is not yet possible to fully explore the data from such reviews. However, having the knowledge of the different definitions not only provides a foundation to build on within the VfM debate, it also enables the knowledge to be progressed to understand how a mechanism can be developed to track the achievement or not of VfM throughout the life of a project.

The VfM debate has been held over many different types of capital build infrastructure project, PPP projects and others, with the most high profile critics being political opposition members who have an inherent duty to decry advances made by their peers, particularly when spending on infrastructure is involved. In such discussions, the argument is usually that a project, build or development has not achieved VfM. The debate never sets out how the VfM is being benchmarked by that critic or how it was or was not tested; neither is it ever explained what the expectations were or where the risks were or even whether the conduct of the stakeholders was to be considered, thus while VfM is debated, with parties taking opposing views, a remarkable observation is that no one can determine categorically how VfM should really be measured. Therefore, the opinions expressed are fundamentally flawed and until the VfM measurement, testing, or tracking mechanism is developed and implemented proactively across projects, to test and track VfM for the benefit or detriment of each stakeholder, there is a lack of contemporaneous evidence.

Testing and tracking

What becomes evident in reviewing the different definitions of VfM, is that while it is important to test the outcome of a project, this test, and the final judgment stating whether a project has achieved a VfM solution or not, should take into consideration all stakeholder perspectives and their aims and objectives for entering into the project in the first instance. This rationale aligns with the ex ante and ex post reviews that are currently advocated from the UK Treasury, in terms of testing the outcome of a project, it does however, also extends that review. By proactively tracking VfM through the lifespan of a project, by all of the stakeholders in collaboration with one another, in practice, this should provide project specific data to allow the reviews to focus on meaningful and contemporaneous data, not political opinion.

By considering the aims and objectives of each stakeholder, which also includes public sector organisations and their individual and collective VfM interests, rather than focusing entirely on a public sector perspective, a level of understanding can be developed that can then produce a foundation from which a tracking mechanism can be built. By approaching VfM in this way, it is possible to see what the vested interests are for each stakeholder, on a project-by-project basis and, of course, what they need to do to achieve individual and collective goals. When these foundations are set out, it is possible to track and test the progress of VfM throughout a project lifespan.

The fluidity of VfM also means that, within a project's life, VfM will periodically fail and succeed as between stakeholders, as inherent project risks arise, are managed and overcome and, again, a tracking mechanism will allow for this to be scrutinised in terms of project and risk management, the allocation of risk and where that sits. Historically, VfM debates tend to rage on, based on limited information, within a particular snapshot of time. A

58 *Tracking VfM*

meaningful mechanism must be developed, not only to identify project- and stakeholder-specific VfM points, but also to allow project critics to have meaningful information to inform debates to determine accurately whether VfM has been achieved or not. In following this path, the VfM debate can be progressed from being a perpetual political whip, to something that becomes a useful mechanism to productively assist in enhancing project performance standards for all stakeholders.

The theory elucidated within this chapter is further developed within the remainder of this book, as each chapter advances the invention of the testing and tracking mechanism.

Notes

1 (Hawkins, Joyce; Allen, Robert, 1991) (Rutherford, 2003)
2 (Rutherford, 2003)
3 (Australian National University, 2018)
4 (Statutes of the Republic of South Africa, 1996)
5 (Statutes of the Republic of South Africa, 1996)

Works cited

Australian National University. (2018). *Value for Money: Budget and Financial Management in the Peoples Republic of China, Taiwan and Australia.* Canberra: Australian National University Press.

Hawkins, J. & Allen, R. (1991). *The Oxford Encyclopaedic English Dictionary.* Oxford : Oxford University Press.

Rutherford, B. (2003). The Social Construction of Financial Statement Elements under Private Finance Initiative Schemes. *Accounting, Auditing and Accountability Journal,* 16, 372–396.

Statutes of the Republic of South Africa. (1996). *Constitution of the Republic of South Africa.* Cape Town: Republic of South Africa Press.

3 Stakeholder roles, responsibilities, expectations, aims, incentives and drivers

The stakeholders to a project are each of the sector-specific participants involved in the purchase, development and use of a project asset, including the funders, those who are expected to work together to create the project, such as the design team, the construction contractor, and facilities or operations management team, and the beneficiaries of the project. These can be listed as:

- Central government
- Local government
- Contractors
- Subcontractors
- Consultants
- Banks and financial institutions
- Beneficiaries.

Sir Michael Latham identified that in order for a win–win solution to be achieved, these sector-specific groups (stakeholders) needed to work in a partnership as a collaborative team and, in order to generate that ethos, many contract documents are drafted with that in mind. Such contracts apportion risk and liability as joint and several obligations with a collective responsibility toward the effective progress of a project. Yet, while this camaraderie of workmanship is expected, it is often not completely accepted by all of the stakeholders, particularly where problems arise. The apportionment of risk in contractual documents soon overrides that partnership ethos and a behavioural pattern of "us and them" often emerges. In order to overcome that entrenched mentality, it is believed that if all participants fully understand the roles, responsibilities, aims and expectations, each of the other, and through project team meetings track their achievement or not of VfM, rather than dividing the team when project risks arise, a mechanism to work cooperatively through the problem times could be developed.

The starting place for this perhaps is to first understand what the fiduciary, legal and governance parameters are for each of the stakeholder groups. This examination of the very different legal and economic interests of each of the stakeholder groups to a project also shows that there are conflicting fiduciary

60   *Stakeholder roles and responsibilities*

duties often between each party, yet positive results can be achieved whilst working collaboratively for a mutually beneficial outcome "where everyone has won and all must have prizes" (Latham, 1994).

Thus, it is essential in any debate about VfM for each of the stakeholder groups to mutually recognise and understand the other and why they have become involved in a project of any kind. This depth of knowledge of each stakeholder's responsibilities, aims and expectations is often set out in individual business planning documents used to justify the reason for proceeding with a project. While the sector-specific reasons for pursuing a project may be significantly different, fundamentally, the driving ambition for a project is for each stakeholder to achieve the aim that they set out to accomplish. This must be the foundation for any VfM test.

Stakeholder roles, responsibilities, expectations and aims

Whilet we have identified the main stakeholders involved in most infrastructure projects above and further classified them in the different subsections below, in order to explore them individually we need to consider them exclusively in further detail. It is often the case that public sector projects involve both central government and local or regional government in a number of roles. The different government roles are or should be distinct and separable, therefore each role is discussed on that basis below.

Central government

Governments, irrespective of their location, be they local, regional or national, have inherent fiduciary duties and statutory roles that are governed usually by both legislative and other policy guidance, in conjunction with historic principles that have evolved over centuries in some cases, often relating to the rule of law (common law or case law decisions) in conjunction with many other cultural philosophies. Such webs of executive, administrative and judicial processes enshrine each country's constitution and where government constitutions might not have such myriad complicated governances, fundamentally, central government has to be accountable.

Predominantly, public accountability and transparent government is the aim of a democratic and free market economy, such mechanisms ensure that the citizens have a number of checks and balances that can be applied to how governments treat their citizens and how its duties are administered. Significantly, while some central governments are not so legislatively controlled, they must still act in the best interests of the its nationals. In the event of discord between government activities and the needs of the populace, mostly the electorate can vote to make changes and even in places where this might be constrained, the ever transparent impact of the internet means that disillusioned and disaffected populations can still vocalise their dissatisfaction, with significant outcomes and potentially

international trade courts can intervene, albeit only in extreme circumstances. It is therefore arguable to state that in a bid to stay in office for as long as possible, central government politicians and civil servants will, as far as possible, act fully and totally in the best interests of the country and the citizens therein. Indeed, in performing its fiduciary duties and acting in the best interests of its citizens, central government must ensure that public money is allocated in accordance with the set national budgetary requirements, as set out within budget statements laid before parliament or a country's democratic or other equivalent mechanism. Individual departments are then tasked with the rolling out the resulting policy within any budgetary limitations.

In terms of the risks to be managed by governments, while they are numerous, one such consideration must be given to the timing of the release of capital infrastructure projects into the market. The construction industry must be able to respond to demand and subsequently deliver projects. Flooding the market with too many projects at the same time could give rise to complications and an adverse impact within the economy. Other risks associated with central government's role are the failure to achieve policy and political requirements, failure to achieve sufficient control of budgets and inadequate monitoring of projects. Indeed the National Audit Office has reprimanded individual departments in the UK for failing to "gather data on project performance, despite clear guidance to do so".

Reputational damage and opposition, or pressure group agitation, sits hand in glove with any high profile failure, irrespective of the colour of the government at the time. Opposition parties are very quick to criticise and public opinion is fickle approaching election time, yet little publicity is given to the successful achievement of the underlying aims and expectations that are evident in many projects.

Central government purchaser

Central government can act in a number of roles during projects. It is often the case that central governments have many different ancillary roles in progressing infrastructure projects. These can include acting as individual funding departments, review boards and scrutineers, purchasers and beneficiaries. Many of the functions established to ensure that there is an improvement in standards, ensure compliance with policy, transparency and anti-competitive practices generating efficiency and monitoring costs. However, when they are acting as purchasers they must do so responsibly.

As a purchaser, central government must act in the same manner as that of local or regional authorities in that it must adhere to either the UNCITRAL Model Law process or the Public Contracts Regulations 2015 processes, or such other procedures depending on which governance document dictates the legislative arena within which it participates as a trading organization.

When purchasing in this role central governments are required, just as any other local or regional authority, to follow the same procedures in assessing the

62 *Stakeholder roles and responsibilities*

viability of undertaking a project. It should, therefore, carry out the options appraisals and scrutiny to understand its "bottom- and top-line figures" and all available options or solutions for the proposed project it is to embark on. The Green Book Analysis, which the UK must follow in this regard, identifies that there are, in normal circumstances, a number of options to consider:

1 Do nothing.
2 Make minor improvements to get to a position that will achieve a goal in the short term, but may not necessarily be a long term or sustainable solution.
3 Undertake more detailed work, with significant investment, but not the optimal solution.
4 Or investment heavily to achieve the required standards of a sustainable solution with a lifecycle to maintain the infrastructure to ensure efficiency.

In order to achieve the options appraisals to this level of detail, however, requires significant time commitment. It is evident from academic texts, and popular culture that "poor pre-planning, promotes poor performance" and that the more detailed work undertaken at this stage, saves a significant amount of time and cost later in the project cycle from all stakeholder perspectives.

Once the options appraisals are undertaken, including scrutiny of the affordability, and financing scenarios and cost consequences, it is then possible to start to collate what aspects of the project are driving each stakeholder's involvement.

Some examples of considerations for the central government purchaser include, electorate needs, public security, political economic strategy, redevelopment and economic growth, society and social health and welfare, educational needs and much more, as identified for each stakeholder in Table 3.1. As is also identified in that table, some of the driving incentives are not necessarily positive ones; or, even more confusingly, some incentives could sit both in a positive and negative position. Irrespective of the positioning of the driving force, it remains a measure that has the impact of moving things forward.

Central government funder

The distinctly different roles undertaken by central government can shift from that of purchaser, as set out above, to that of funder. The funding often provided by central government being either equity or revenue financing, this change of remit sees a dramatic shift in how projects are viewed, giving rise to entirely different elements of aims and expectations. The overriding duty however for central government must be to ensure that national government policy is adhered to and is progressed and the interests of its citizens are preserved.

The ability for central government to provide funding comes in many guises be it allocation of national funds from the national public purse or of

Table 3.1 Key drivers or incentives of each stakeholder group involvement

Central government		Local government		Private sector contractor		Financier (debt and equity)		Beneficiary group employees		Beneficiary group service user	
+ve driver	-ve driver	+ve driver	-ve driver	+ve driver	-ve driver	+ve driver	-ve driver	+ve driver	-ve driver	+ve driver	-ve driver
Policy achievement	Budgets	Policy	Budgets	Profit	Cost of bid	Profit	Outlay not recovered	Improved working environment	Constant problems	Improved service provision	Increased council tax
Investment capital asset	Reputation	Investment capital asset	Accessible funding solutions	Kudos	Risk management	Low risk investment	Step in mitigation required	Efficient technology	Inefficient solutions	Improved service facilities	Legacy not sustainable
Economic growth	Political risk	Local economic growth	Cost	Future opportunities	Loss or profit	Business growth and development	Contract termination	Efficient and sustainable environmental solutions	Poor environmental solution	Improved environment	
Sustainable solutions	Willing to pay	Sustainable solutions	Reputational risk	Business growth and development	Reputational damage	Future opportunities		Cost savings	Increased cost	Generation of wellbeing and pride	
Healthy balance sheets		Improved service provisions	Political risk	Healthy balance sheet				Wellbeing and positive workable working environment	Poor attainment	Improving opportunity	

Improved service provision	Achievement of community growth and development	Willing to pay	Achievement of award and enhanced reputation within industry Elevation of competitive edge	Creativity	Inflexible environment	Willing to pay
Legacy	Legacy		Corporate strategy and vision	Income generation	Loss of productivity	Willing to use
National strategy	Local strategy					Community enhancement

aid and grant contributions, from external sources, or providing loans from public sector sources such as the Public Works Loan Board (PWLB). In the UK, local government has been able to obtain loans from the PWLB since 2004. Prior to that time, local authorities had to seek parliamentary approval. Even now the application for the loan must be undertaken in accordance with the legislative guidelines, the "Prudential Code" and other applicable accounting regulations. This form of borrowing for the public sector, also referred to as prudential borrowing, is often less expensive than the form of loans available within the wider market. The interest payable on the PWLB is set by the UK Treasury, rather than the Bank of England, which sets the base rate against which other banks benchmark their own interest rates. In this role, central government's drivers and incentives relate to the fiscal position of the country in which they operate.

Balancing books in a country with a longstanding deficit, where expenditure outstrips GDP, can be quite a challenging task. However, in cases where the country is affluent, the challenges show in different guises. Indeed, it could be said that the VfM challenge for an affluent country is just as difficult as that in a poorer country. The risks for any financier sit in its ability to recover its initial outlay and, of course, the interest thereon to ensure that it is profiting from its service. Often there are many risks, particularly within infrastructure projects that could hinder the financier's ability to recover its debt; it is for this reason that banks and central government often want to impose contractual requirements into projects within which they become involved. These often include the right to step into the works if the contractor become insolvent or requiring any funds supplied by them to be held in escrow or a designated bank account, which cannot be "contaminated" by other funding to enable the money to be ringfenced for an exact purpose. These tools enable the funders to in part protect their investment.

In progressing the review of what issues incentivises and drives the differing arms of the "public body" into a project, the next role that should be considered is that of scrutineer.

Central government scrutineer

Primarily, the role of scrutineers was established to protect national government policy and ensure fiduciary obligations were implemented throughout the procurement and development of a project. The mechanisms used to undertake this role includes ensuring that projects are initiated properly by ensuring that the appropriate business case considerations have been investigated, that the appropriate governance and impact assessments have been undertaken at the different stages of a project. Central government, as part of this process, sets out processes and procedures that must be followed. These are often commenced through a reporting process. In the first instance, the UK scrutineers, which often sit with Cabinet Office, require the production of a project initiation document as a starting document, from that, as the proposed project becomes more of a reality, an outline business

66 *Stakeholder roles and responsibilities*

case is required and, eventually, a final business case; within each document at each stage of a project there has to be evidence that, to continue the project, the project must achieve a VfM solution. The obvious flaw with this process is that these reviews are often carried out at the front end of the project, when VfM cannot be fully measured, aims, objectives and a methodology can be proposed to show how the aims and objectives are to be achieved is the only document that can be produced at the inception of a project, a business case, options appraisal and then finally a decision.

Once a project has commenced, there is no tracking system, in spite of the fact that the UK has a look-back test, there is no prescribed method of scrutiny to undertake that kind of review from a central government perspective or even a local government perspective. However, it is also held that the benefit of this scrutiny mechanism is related to the perception of central government's role by the other stakeholder groups. Contracting authorities see this involvement as being "protectionist". Both local government and contractors use the arms' length distance of central government to provide an element of independence and, in some instances, as commercial leverage.

Local government

Local government purchaser

In the UK, the local authority's financial affairs have to be administered properly under the watchful eye of the s. 151 officer, as created by s.151 of the Local Government Act 1972. Interestingly, it becomes the responsibility of authority finance officers (set out within the Green Book as at 2003) to ensure VfM is achieved. Ultimately, local authorities must act in the best interests of the communities and the people within them whom they serve and who pay into the taxation system, by whatever means.

The key drivers and incentives for the investment and participation by a local authority is akin to that of central government. Yet, by the same measure, its role is distinctly different. Central government must adhere to national policy giving consideration to its country as a whole, whereas a local authority is driven by concerns at a local level. The role of the local authority within a project is also potentially subject to constraints emitting from central government policy and guidance. The legislative parameters within which UK local authorities are governed, from both a financial and governance perspective are set out within Local Government Act provisions and financial regulation provisions.

Local government's expectations are set out on a project-by-project basis in accordance with their corporate strategy and from a micro-perspective from the business plans and feasibility studies that are undertaken as part of the project process (Bing, Akintoye & Edwards, 2005).

While they have similar fiduciary duties to central government, they have less control over the timing of the projects and the accessibility to finance. It is acknowledged that local authorities are often constantly being squeezed in terms of budgets by central government. Their electorate have demands and expectations for better quality services and provision while the budgets to provide the services required are being eroded (Braun, 2001), ever more so since the 2008 financial market collapse with many authorities in the UK expected to make 40% savings, as against their budgets, until 2017. Local authorities are being encouraged to be innovative in the solutions they employ to achieve their functions yet their changing constitutional role fetters the flexibility required to carry this out (Jowell & Oliver, 2004).

In planning local authority budgets and departmental needs, not just in the UK, each local authority is required to carry out, in accordance with various statutory requirements, or even simply common sense planning requirements, a review of what they will need to spend in the next financial year. All entities that find themselves in a position of austerity must make decisions about cost savings. Local authorities have services that they are statutorily bound to undertake and they also perform roles and undertake services that are not statute based. It is evident that in an economic downturn and when budgets are significantly reduced, statutory and frontline services override the need, for example to repair or replace a roof that could last another year or so and this position will not be isolated to the UK. Indeed sometimes decisions are taken that result in buildings being mothballed. HMT, within its various publications, has highlighted that this in fact is what, over a number of decades, has been happening to infrastructure within the UK. Over the last 40 years buildings and infrastructure have been left or simply not maintained. HMT incentives to replace, refurbish and repair infrastructure by offering additional sources of finance, is in the case of some local authorities, the push which is needed to drag them out of Victorian times into a modern 21st-Century world.

As previously stated, a contracting authority's role within society has undergone changes (Jowell & Oliver, 2004; Bult-Spiering & Dewult, 2006) over the last few years. The erosion of their functions has left them in a situation where, whether they realise it or not, they are the developers within their communities (ibid.). This development function is the role they perform in pursuing the course of a project.

Fundamentally, the primary considerations for contracting authorities are many and far reaching. Therefore, their expectations in pursuing a project and committing significant financial resources into an investment, should be to achieve connected outputs and not simply the reconstruction of a building. Indeed, if government intervention has been deemed necessary in order to procure the capital infrastructure project, then it is appropriate that government expectations would incorporate the requirement to fulfil the following objectives:

- Their statutory function, demands from their external stakeholders and arms' length organisations would require a beneficial outcome for connected communities.

68 *Stakeholder roles and responsibilities*

- Their need to survive in the future and what shape and function that will be would require positive and successful achievement of a project.
- Their growing competitive arena policy objectives of their local electorate while dovetailing with central government and legislative constraints.
- Budgeting appropriately to ensure that resources are maintained to not only achieve a successful conclusion of a project but not to distract from continuing to provide ongoing frontline services.
- Balancing the books during the procurement process and for the whole life of the project, which is ever more pertinent in austere times.
- Negotiating the best deal commercially and ensuring that the best and most up-to-date advice is available.
- Not acting ultra vires in any of the decisions made.
- Keeping their stakeholders informed and onboard.
- Ongoing contract management and achievement of continuous improvement in line with best value legislation.
- Development of local economy and employment opportunities.

Bearing in mind all of the above that the local authority assessment of VfM will inevitably mirror the HMT processes, there would be additional expectations to be delivered including but not limited to:

- not raising the profile of the authority in a negative way
- avoiding bad publicity
- providing innovative and bespoke solutions that will entrench a feeling of pride within the community and fulfilling user satisfaction.

Having investigated the public sector and administrative roles, expectations and aims it is necessary to balance the debate to investigate the roles, aims and expectations of the other stakeholder groups.

Private sector

Private sector funders

The role of private sector funders, while not dissimilar to that of the public sector funders, in terms of the applying an interest rate to the amount of borrowing, their main raison d'être is to make a profit for its shareholders and, while the economy and stability of a particular country's economy has a bearing on the private sector financier's performance, it is the need to keep the shareholders happy that drives the investment aims and objectives.

In previous sections, the roles and expectations of the public sector and private sector contractors have been reviewed to enable a comparative analysis to be undertaken. Table 3.1 also incorporates the funders in order to review and compare what the funders' incentives and drivers are. Not unlike the private sector contractor, there is very little literature about this topical arena. Significantly, the information has been provided through attendance at the International Project Finance Association seminars.

The main area of criticism in relation to funders is that they are seen to be one of the main cause of delay to the financial close of deals and that they gain the most from any deal while bearing little of the risk. Primarily, they do what they are good at, they are:

- Providing the money up front adding an interest rate to reflect the risk profile of the project depending on the debt funding structure used by the parties to obtain an affordable deal.
- Accepting that if the project contract for whatever reason goes wrong, they will step into the contract to sort it out, or put it into administration.
- Collecting the repayment.
- Supporting refinance.

The above list is, however, an oversimplification of their role during the process of the project deal. The funder's advisors carry out a significant amount of due diligence not just in terms of the commercial points within the deal, but in terms of the project's risk profile (from their own perspective) (Akintoye et al., 2001). As a secondary outcome to this process, local authorities gain a level of comfort as they see it as a form of "doubling checking" their position. Local authorities understand that if anything goes wrong, the banks will step in first to protect their own interest, but, in so doing, the authority perceives this as being an additional layer of protection.

Based on the above position, it could be argued that it would be quite a simple task to determine where the funders to each deal achieve their VfM point or achieve their aims, objectives and key drivers.

Private sector contractor and subcontractors (including professional advisors)

The next stakeholder group is that of the contractor (the entity providing the goods, works or services, being the subject matter of the project) and, for the purposes of this scenario, we will relate the contractor to private sector entities. The private sector entities within a project can be numerous, based on project-specific needs, for example in a construction project that utilises a traditional design, build, finance and operate process will be represented by a number of stakeholders, for the purposes of this research the focus will be on the contractors, from both the perspective of the construction and operations, and the funders, being both debt and equity providers (PPP, 2015). Literature sources highlight that the biggest beneficiaries of projects are the contractors and advisors for each of the projects; what fails to be debated academically within the built environment (or otherwise) is that the ultimate beneficiaries are the service users and it is for this reason that this chapter focuses on their needs. For the purposes of this

70 Stakeholder roles and responsibilities

research, the service users are the employees, and infrastructure users of the infrastructure project. For example, the service users of schools are the pupils, employees and the wider community, who utilise the building or the project facility, and thereby, each member of that beneficiary group derives a significant benefit therefrom. Ultimately, the facility is procured for use by the beneficiary as end user. On this basis, the stance that the service users should be the most important "beneficiary" for the purposes of any project is fundamental in assessing VfM. After all, they are the ones who assist in measuring compliance with performance standards, by responding to the contractor's customer satisfaction surveys, which are issued often in accordance with inbuilt contractual requirements.

Private sector contractors

Inherently, the projects that are undertaken are undertaken to redevelop, replace or rebuild public sector infrastructure (Henjewele, Sun & Fewings, 2011). The projects are high value in nature, involve medium- to long-term commitments (depending on the stakeholder group) and often high profile quality projects, providing the opportunity to work with some of the best teams in the industry. In terms of risks within the project, while the private sector has high risk at the front end of the project, the risk profile diminishes at different key stages (Gao & Handley-Schlacher, 2002). The opportunities for the private sector to profit under the contract are varied and arise as a result of a number of inherent factors within the project structures, throughout the contractual period.

Some projects are risky because of their very nature, as design, build, finance, operate contracts inherently involve the construction industry as a whole, not just the building contractor but the whole sector from the architectural design through to the wider design teams, specialist trades, suppliers of goods as well as services and facilities management teams (Arewa, 2011). As the contracts also involve the element of finance, the wider economic impact of such contracts involves the finance industry and again it is not simply the banks or fund management companies that become involved but also specialist accountants and advisors. Lawyers are also a necessity within this process irrespective of the drive to minimise the cost of legal fees through the use of the standard form contracts.

It has been said that these kinds of infrastructure project have created their own industry (Whitfield, 2001) and on the face of it, that is true but the rationale for the private sector contractor entering into such a market is based on profitability. This assertion is supported by Rutherford (2003), who refers to contractors as profit seeking. Private sector contractors tend not to be in business for altruistic reasons and with that in mind they are rarely corporately registered as having charitable status. The provisions of the Companies Act (2006) require that directors of a corporate entity act in the best interests of the company. The best interests of a company are predominantly served by the aims and objectives of the company to engage in a profitable business. Thus, the directors' fiduciary duty is to the company and its shareholders (Lim, 2013). Their incentives and driving forces are based entirely on the goal of profit. However, there are very few academic or available industry documents that set out the incentives for the contractor's business. The main reports within which this information can be found are the business, strategy and development plans undertaken by contracting entities but these are rarely to be found in the public domain.

If profit is the main incentive for entering into a project, then the establishment of an appropriate profit margin is paramount. This is understood by the public sector when projects are put out to the market. Therefore, if the contract is sufficiently high value and high profile, there will be healthy contractor interest in the development. The driving force is the ability to make money from the project and also the reputational gain achieved from successfully completing a high profile project. This could be deemed to give a competitive edge when considering bidding for future equivalent projects, particularly in times of recession when projects become scarce.

High value projects however, often come with high value risks (NAO, 2010). While the ethos of such private financing projects has been, "whoever is best able to manage the risk, should bear the risk", such risks have predominantly sat with the contractor for the life of the contract but at a cost. It is not unreasonable, therefore, to anticipate that the expectation by the private sector is that the rewards they reap should be proportionate to the risk taken. However, Roy (2011) highlights that, in order to address VfM issues, the element of risk should be redistributed; he maintains that it should still be managed by the party best able to deal with it, but this might now be the role in some circumstances of the authority, not that of the contractor. Arguably, this was always the UK government mantra as evidenced within the different versions of the Green Book, but the risk has not necessarily been passed back to the public sector.

It is argued that it is the accounting treatment of how projects are balanced on the UK's books that determines where the risk should sit as on-balance sheet position, rather than an off-balance sheet (HMT, 2008), as this would have an impact on the country's financial profile and status.

In assessing the private sector's expectations, it can be assumed that they aim to do the best job they can for their client, finish the job on time and within the profit margins set and to provide a quality design, build and continued service worthy of recognition, recommendation and enhanced reputation. They do not want to alienate their supply chain or their funding consortia and they need to keep their shareholders and directors happy. These expectations and drivers are also set out within the Table 3.1 to allow a comparison of each stakeholder group. These drivers and incentives are also borne out within the contracts into which they enter. Therefore, their

72 *Stakeholder roles and responsibilities*

aims and expectations are governed by the commercial deal or bargain reached (Kaming et al., 1997).

The summary to be drawn at this stage is that, while each party to the project has many different driving forces, it could be said, after that all parties are aiming to achieve most, if not all, of the objective and subjective VfM principles.

However, strategically, they are pursuing this by different means that suit their own individual and conflicting purposes, although targeting a collective benefit or goal.

Arguably, the complex ever changing facets of projects (Henjewele et al., 2011) when analysed against the differing expectations of each of the parties, are part of the reason why establishing a one-size-fits-all VfM test to determine whether projects provide VfM in the procurement of capital build projects is impossible, as each project must be assessed on its own merit. However, the societal expectations change in terms of what is acceptable and demand furthermore fluctuation is shown significantly by virtue of what the user is willing to pay for and what it is willing to accept. Therefore, establishing a mechanism to test VfM across each stakeholder group is problematic but not unachievable.

The next section considers the position of the funders as a stakeholder group and where their drivers may be.

Beneficiaries as a stakeholder group

The beneficiary groups are the main recipients of a benefit, in accordance with the ordinary meaning of "beneficiary" (Oxford Encyclopaedic Dictionary), from a project perspective, the beneficiaries can also be numerous but for the purposes of this exercise, we will term them to be the end users. However, the beneficiaries as a group are wide and varied. While many critics state that the main beneficiaries are the financiers, consultants and other advisors (Freer, 2004), because they are alleged to make the most money out of a public sector infrastructure project, these, as a beneficiary group, should not be the main consideration. As far as this book is concerned, there has been very little consideration given to the real beneficiaries of projects, such as the end user, the community benefit and ultimate gain to society, although the economic benefit of construction is widely accepted and acknowledged within many scholarly and government papers (BIS, 2013)

In reality, not all beneficiary groups have much interest at the foundation or feasibility stage of a project. Higher level management and stakeholder beneficiaries will input into the process and will be kept informed of decisions and developments in pulling together feasibility plans and business cases. The ultimate user groups, at this initial stage, may have little interest in such developments. Significantly, communities and end users tend to have a resistance to change generally, even when it is for the better and often initially perceive the change as a detrimental step (Dent & Galloway-Goldberg, 1999).

Stakeholder roles and responsibilities 73

However, it can be argued that, the beneficiaries are a large and varied number of people, who are affected at various stages of the project. They can be divided into two main categories, i.e. public sector decision makers and the tax-paying public. Unfortunately, there is very little literature available to analyse in terms of beneficiary group benefits or detriments in the context of project studies. The beneficiary element does not appear to be debated and whether the beneficiaries achieve VfM, from being involved in a capital build project is difficult to determine and depends on the key stage of the procurement process and on the category of beneficiary that is involved at each of those key stages. The two main categories of beneficiary can be subdivided into narrow beneficiary groups as set out below. The main reasons for dividing the beneficiary groups up this way are to highlight that:

(I) The public sector decision makers determine, on behalf of the beneficiaries, what capital project it pursues, or requires government intervention. As we have seen above, invariably this is linked to a national agenda, societal failing or other national determinant; whereas

(II) The tax-paying public has no real choice as to how or why these projects should be procured, apart from a vote at the ballot box in the next general or local election.

(III) Each of the beneficiaries is also considered within different sections of society or local community within which a large capital build development project takes place. In order to ascertain the beneficiaries to a project, the list for the beneficiaries has been divided into four narrower categories:

- The local authority and other stakeholders
- The service providers (local authority employees)
- The service users
- The wider community (including the employees of contractors).

Fundamentally, the significance of the breakdown of the beneficiary groups is to enable a determination of where to set the VfM point or measurement and that essentially is governed by which group is being represented. For the purposes of this book, it was initially necessary to consider the overall benefits derived by each beneficiary group, but then the research was narrowed to the service users and employees based within the new facilities. The rationale for this was that the public sector position already reflected the benefits to the local authority, (including other stakeholders) and service providers, (which tend to be other public sector groups). As expressed above, the service users tend to input in a more limited way, pursuant to underlying, contractual requirements and the related assessment of the contractor's performance.

Local authority and other stakeholders ultimately derive a benefit through having a valuable tangible asset that they can use in the future to drive either an income or provide an enhanced service to the benefit of the wider community.

74 *Stakeholder roles and responsibilities*

The service providers derive a benefit from the up-to-date and often advanced technology, design and build techniques to make their working environment more user friendly and cost efficient. The service providers will have been engaged in the design elements of defining the output specification required of the building, scoping the services needed and ultimately signing off the design.

Arguably, the benefits gained by local communities can be identified throughout the period of a project from a short-, medium- and long-term perspective, the long-term plans having yet to be realised from the majority of projects that are long-term deals that have been entered into over a finance period of 25–30 years as many design, build, finance and operate contracts are.

The short-term benefits during the planning phase are that interest groups, be they supportive or otherwise, ensure that local people come together as a community and are able to express an opinion where necessary. From this involvement, the community interest, awareness and involvement begin. The medium-term benefits to the local economies are often derived from an influx of construction workers in an area for a prolonged period of time of a build project. Local cafes and retail businesses during this period thrive in the support given to these workers admittedly for a narrow period of time. Once the project is built, the beneficiary groups change again and the aims of the long-term benefits and the raison

d'être for the project in the first place starts to progress.

Within each of the key stages of the procurement process, throughout the build phase of the project and beyond, there are inevitably sectors of society who will, for a brief period of time, perhaps suffer a detriment and that will always be inevitable, even with the smallest of projects. The ultimate test, from a beneficiary perspective, is the power over payment and use in some circumstances. If beneficiaries are willing to pay for the new infrastructure, and they use it for its intended purposes, then it can be deemed to have achieved its goal. Beneficiaries tend not to be too concerned about the cost, unless, that is, the impact of the infrastructure is either unaffordable and they cannot pay to use the provision. Or if the consequence is an increase in taxation above than what might be deemed to be reasonably acceptable. Beneficiaries, ultimately, are concerned about the quality of the end result, the ease and comfort of use, the effect it has on communities and community relationships. Fundamentally, does it do what it was supposed to do, irrespective of the cost? Table 3.1 identifies some of the key drivers and incentives that influence the stakeholders in making their decisions about whether they are to pursue a project or not.

Summary

It is also appropriate to consider within this debate where the risk and reward lie, because in giving consideration to the elements of risk and the reward to be achieved, the rewards, which may equate to the stakeholder expectations to be achieved and are secured, can be linked to the successful investment in infrastructure. Successful capital investments will give rise to a growth in the ability to compete within a worldwide market economy (BIS, 2013). Such investment also provides short-, medium- and long-term benefits to local communities and economies not just to the national strategic goals (Awuzie & McDermott, 2013).

But it is not simply a matter of having each of the stakeholder groups acknowledge this position, it is also necessary for the UK construction industry council step toward this aim; they developed a services specification in 2007, which set out all the services required from every stakeholder within a design team, intending that this information would sit within a contract document. Unfortunately, it would seem that this did not become a best practice specification for design team service contracts. One explanation for this lack of uptake is that the insurance industry for the construction industry would not provide insurance against a specification that lists each duty for each discipline within a design team. The rationale being that this would give rise to additional risk, liability and cost being imposed on one as against another disproportionately or unreasonably. In any event, it was a starting point to address the notion that each stakeholder group within a project should have an understanding of each other's expectations, needs and aims for the project. It is the case on a practical level that each stakeholder does understand the roles, duties and obligations of the other, and to a certain extent the drivers and incentives of each stakeholder on a generic basis, but it is acknowledged within the industry that the knowledge does not go far enough on a project-by-project basis.

Table 3.1 goes some way to try to demystify what those incentives and drivers are for each of the stakeholder groups. Identified within the table are both positive and negative elements for each stakeholder group. Having broken down the incentives and drivers in this way, it is evident that while there are some conflicting reasons for a stakeholder group's involvement, there are also a number of converging incentives and drivers that are carried across all stakeholder groups. In understanding where these elements sit and by setting out in the early course of a project what the realistic expectations are for the project, for each of the projects stages of development, as distinct from the incentives and drivers, for each of the stakeholder groups, this allows the foundations to be set and a methodology for achieving a VfM tracking mechanism to be implemented.

Having established the project goals, aims and expectations for each stakeholder at a very early stage allows, on a project-by-project basis, the identification of where each stakeholder is able to achieve their own VfM point, and also to identify at any given point within a project where and with whom the risks associated with the project sit. It also assists where, for whatever reason, VfM is not being achieved, in the understanding of why it is not to allow for mitigation if necessary and or provides the information that shows while VfM is not currently being achieved because of X factor at this given time, when the risk shifts or is overcome, or other intervention is injected into then the VfM will catch up and be achieved at a further point

76 *Stakeholder roles and responsibilities*

along the project journey. If you recall, in Chapter 2 it is acknowledged that VfM is fluid and there will inevitably within any project be a rise and fall in its attainment. It is unrealistic to expect projects to be VfM throughout their development journey for everyone.

Works cited

Akintoye, A., Hardcastle, C., Beck, M. & Chinyio, E. (2001). *The Financial Structure of Private Finance Initiative Projects*. Manchester: Association of Researchers in Construction Management.

Awuzie, B. & McDermott, P. (2013). *JVS and Partnership: Towards Organising for Viable Infrastructure Delivery in Developing Countries*. Preston: University of Central Lancashire Press.

Bing, L., Akintoye, A. & Edwards, P. (2005). The Allocation of Risk in PPP/PFI Construction Projects in the UK. *International Journal of Project Management*, 23, 25–35.

Braun, P. (2001). *The Practical Impact of EU Public Procurement Law on PFI Practice in the UK. PhD from*Nottingham University.

Bult-Spiering, M. & Dewult, G. 2006. *Strategic Issues in Public Private Partnerships: an International Perspective*. Oxford: Blackwell.

Dent, E.B. & Galloway-Goldberg, S. (1999). Challenging Resistance to Change. *Applied Behavioural Science*, 35, 25–41.

Freer, R. (2004). A Private View of PFI. *ICE- Civil Engineering*, 157.

Gao, S.S. & Handley-Schlacher, M. (2002). Public Bodies Perceptions of Risk Transfer in the UK's PFI. *Journal of Finance and Management in Public Services*, 3.

Henjewele, C., Sun, M. & Fewings, P. (2011). Critical Parameters Influencing VfM Variations in PFI Projects in the Healthcare and Transport Sectors. *Construction Management and Economics*, 29, 825–839.

Jowell, J. & Oliver, D. (2004). *The Changing Constitution*. Oxford: Oxford University Press.

Kaming, P., Olomoaiye, P., Holt, G. & Harris, F. (1997). Factors Influencing Construction Time and Cost Over-run in High Rise Projects in Indonesia. *Construction Management and Economics*, 15, 83–94.

Latham, M. (1994). *Constructing the Team*, London: Her Majesty's Stationery Office.

4 Identification of the value for money stages

Where VfM might arise: the key stages

Liu et al. (2013) debated where VfM points could be identified when trying to ascertain a practical tool for the measurement of performance in construction, which they called a Performance Measurement Framework (PMF). This PMF worked on the basis of understanding the key stakeholders, which is not unlike the analysis undertaken within Chapter 3 of this book. Further attempts to identify where VfM points arise took the form of the Performance Prism, created by Neely, Gregory and Platts. Neely et al. stated that there were five distinct components to the identification process, including stakeholder satisfaction, strategies and processes. However, the mechanism suggested herein highlights that there could be at least nine different key stages and maybe more. The key stages are variable depending on the type of project being undertaken, the procurement process being followed and the stakeholders involved. For the purpose of this book a typical design and build construction project is being used as the example. Therefore, the stages can be broken down into the nine distinct elements. Each of the stages is discussed below.

The feasibility stage: key stage 1

The feasibility stage will be undertaken by the majority of the participants, this is the business planning element of any project, which will determine whether the project is worth pursuing. The individual stakeholders will undertake their own project assessments on the limited information that they are likely to have at this time, to consider a number of key questions and concerns that would need to be addressed in any form of feasibility study, while public sector stakeholders are likely to consider soft questions such as:

1 Is the project needed, what are the alternative options?
2 Is it in the public interest and will it be popular?
3 Is going to be cost effective?
4 Is the project linked to income generation and is it a statutory requirement?

78 Identification of the VfM stages

5 How will it benefit the community?
6 What are the risks of doing the project, of not doing the project or created during the project?
7 What are the benefits and to whom?
8 What is the short-term pain; what is the long-term gain?
9 How much will it cost? Can it be done? Can the facility be kept open during the works/services?
10 Impact on communities from a negative perspective during the process?
11 Will the end user return once completed if they have found an alternative?
12 How much will they be prepared to pay?

Public sector stakeholders also equally need to address hard questions, based on tangible facts. Thus, the feasibility appraisal format is also set out in Green Book guidance, which has been further developed by Her Majesty's Treasury (HMT) in the UK and extended into the "Public Sector Business Cases using the Five Case Model: A Toolkit". This toolkit advocates that each feasibility study or business plan should include the following essential sets of information:

the strategic case
the economic case
the commercial case
the financial case
the management position.

Not only should the questions above be answered in the development of each of the sections, but further questions should also be considered, such as:

a What are my expectations for this project during the process and when it completes (if it goes ahead)?
b Are they realistic expectations at each juncture?

In order to address each individual stakeholder perspective, it is necessary for each to communicate its expectations to the others during the process. Arguably, this is undertaken in every project during the procurement process and contractual negotiations. Yet, realistically, the issues addressed during that period often do not reflect every stakeholder's expectations, fully. Therefore, as soon as the expectation is not met, projects are criticised for not being VfM, irrespective of actuality. Thus, the UK HMT toolkit should be extended further and address the matters advocated within this text to include sections relating to the matters as below.

Identification of the VfM stages 79

Design expectations

Everyone has an idea about what they would like or what they think they would like to see in terms of the design of the development. These features should be discussed and developed in collaboration with each other. One would argue that this already happens. The introduction and use of BIM modelling assists in this process; and the showcasing of ideas to the public often happens, but the expected outcome for each of the stakeholders is not fully captured. Thus, while the architect and purchaser may have one set of expectations, the contractor and subcontractors may have a different set of expectations, for that particular phase of a project. In terms of design, con-tractors often are not yet engaged. Therefore, it is feasible that contractors as the design development stage, as a key tracking stage to state that they have no expectations. The contractor considerations, during the feasibility stage may well be identified as:

1 Is it in the company's interests to pursue the project?
2 Is it cost effective?
3 Will it be publicly popular?
4 Can we showcase from it to generate a good image and reputation?
5 What are the risks of doing the project?
6 What are the risks of not doing the project?
7 What are the costs associated with the project?
8 Do I need to source finance?
9 Who will pay for the product once completed?
10 What are the finance risks and associated costs?
11 Is the potential client an intelligent client?

With additional considerations to be given to contractor specific expecta-tions such as:

a What do we expect from this project?
b What profit margin do I need to apply?
c What level of risk do I anticipate I should carry?
d Do I need to recruit and or pay additional bonus?
e What supply chain conditions will I need?
f How do I control that?
g What is the availability of resources?
h What is the current economic climate?
i What is my competition?
j What design risks are there likely to be during the project?
k What kind of contract is to be used?
l Is the client an intelligent client?
m Are they likely to change their minds?
n What is the likelihood of client delay?

80 *Identification of the VfM stages*

o   Is the project high profile?
p   Will it win awards?
q   Is it a popular project?
r   Does it have public support?
s   Does it have stakeholder buy in?
t   Are there any pressure groups opposing this project?
u   Does it have planning consent?
v   What are the risk factors to the site (underground and overground)?
w   What are the waste considerations and environmental risk factors?
x   What contingencies do we need?
y   How long will the procurement process take?
z   How much will the procurement process cost as an upfront and unrecoverable sum if we do not win the project?
aa Is there sufficient time for the delivery or is the client being unrealistic?

Each of the expectations or questions can be subdivided into the different key stages, which can then be tracked.

The funder will have questions such as:

1   Is this project worth investing in?
2   Is the contractor capable of performing the works to the required standard?
3   Is the contracting entity able to repay the debt?
4   What rating will be applied?
5   What is the level of equity to debt?
6   What are the applicable interest rates?
7   How long will the money be tied up for?
8   What contractual provisions will be in place to protect the money?
9   Is it income generating?

Finally, the beneficiary, as the end user, will also have questions, although it is unlikely that they will develop a business case at the outset. The beneficiary VfM points are only likely to be traceable if a marketing or opinion poll is taken particularly in the early stages. Customer satisfaction surveys are often carried out but this is usually at the final stage (stage9), when the project is complete. Nonetheless, the beneficiary to a project often has questions that should be considered, perhaps as part of the feasibility and the ongoing construction phase of any infrastructure project. These will include matters such as:

1   How is this going to impact on my daily life?
2   Is it for the best that this happens?
3   Are there going to be any negative consequences during the project?
4   Are they outweighed by the benefit of the end result?
5   How long will the project take?

6 What are the detriments that I am going to suffer?
7 Will I be compensated?
8 What are my alternatives; will that be at an increased cost?
9 What is the difference in cost for the new provision?
10 How much is my tax going to increase to support this venture?

All of the above questions for each of the stakeholder groups are variable and actual responses will inevitably be influenced by numerous different project events.

The biggest fluctuation in response will probably sit with both the public sector purchaser and the contractor, as the risk profile of any project will fluctuate between the two parties as the project develops. Inevitably there are always risks associated with all parts of a project and consequently there will be an impact on the expectations of each stakeholder. The impact could be either a positive or a negative impact. The analogy being to that of Newton's Cradle, in that for every action there is likely to be a positive and or negative reaction.

The workability of the VfM tracking mechanism requires that the expectations are disclosed to the parties at the outset of the process and there is no reason why this cannot take place. Individually each stakeholder group will have worked through the feasibility stage to get to position of undertaking or taking part in the key stage 2 process, being the procurement process and, in doing so, they will have determined what their individual expectations are.

The procurement process: key stage 2

Thus for key stage 2, being the procurement process, the expectations arising from this stage would be:

1 The procuring entity: public sector:
2 to find a preferred bidder who can deliver the project and the requirements of the authority

b and, in order to achieve that outcome, the public sector stakeholder would expect to undertake a number of tasks, to provide sufficient information to the market to enable the interested bidders an opportunity to bid for the work. Therefore, they would need to collate all necessary information to facilitate the preparation of the bid documents. This information would include:

i site information, including plans and any title information
ii a vision or architects brief for the outputs expected from the infrastructure, scope and objectives
iii a summary of the background to the proposed development including details perhaps of local socioeconomic, political and geographical demographics

82 *Identification of the VfM stages*

iv   the procurement documents, questions, scoring criteria including evaluation methodology, programme of bid process

v   contract documents and financial information so far as possible.

It is also highly likely that in order to get to this level of detail the public sector stakeholder will have invested a significant sum of money and time in gathering this information together. It may well be that, once the information is collated, the procuring authority will want to see if there is sufficient interest within the market for the private sector to want to undertake the work. With this in mind, the authority may seek to hold a market testing day, to promote the event and to start to generate interest in the project by informing the market that this exciting project is "coming soon".

Once this information has been put out to the market and the process commenced, the public sector stakeholder will then need to ensure that there are identified panel members available to undertake evaluations once the bid documents have been submitted, that there is sufficient resource to monitor any clarification questions and channel communications in a transparent manner. The risk that sits with this process for the public sector procuring entity is quite significant. Irrespective of the amount of work that a procuring entity may undertake at this stage, it is not always the case that a procurement will generate a lot of market interest or result in the return of enough bids to hold a competitive process. The procuring entity then has to make further decisions about whether they should progress or wait until such a time that the market is in a better position to respond.

The expectations of the contractors for the duration and outcome of the key stage 2: procurement process would be to undertake a bid process cost effectively and, if successful, to proceed through the next stage to contract/financial close. Not unlike the procuring stakeholder, in order to get through this process, the contractor expects to have to invest time and money to pursuing this competition. Once the bid documents are put to the market, the contractor has only a limited time within which to prepare any submission responses. In progressing this procurement, there may well be a need for the contractor to visit a number of sites, perhaps test the ground and carry out surveys to ensure that so far as possible, when it comes to developing a price, as many risks and issues have been identified, so that a realistic cost can be priced for the project. In conjunction with site visits, there may well need to be meetings arranged with architects and other design team members to quantify any potential work. The procuring entity may have agreed to meet with the bidders either collectively or individually to respond to any questions, to allow clarification of issues to be addressed; and to enable the bidders the opportunity to further understand what the procuring entities expectations are, but usually only to a limited extent.

Losing bidders, depending on the project and the process undertaken, would view the process as being just another hurdle to overcome, unless the procuring entity had erred in its process and taken too long or acted in

Identification of the VfM stages 83

breach of any of the procurement conditions adopted by the procuring entity and, in such an event, a losing bidder could avail himself of any mechanism to obtain redress.

It would be expected that each of the participants would work through with the procuring entity systematically for each of the milestones to identify in their individual cases what they are expecting to achieve from each stage. As this is an individual stakeholder group exercise there can be no right or wrong answer. The further milestones for this exercise are as follows.

The preferred bidder phase: key stage 3

During this phase the expectations, and contractual requirements should be being finalised, finetuned and commitments to the project confirmed. It is from this point that the VfM tracking mechanism will start to move for the majority of stakeholders, the winning bidder will obviously see a positive shift in its mechanism because it has won the bid. The contracting authority will also see a positive advance in its mechanism because it is beginning its journey to achieve its goal. In terms of the financiers, however, they may see a negative dip arising from a positive result, purely because they may need to prepare to release money that at this point they will not be making a gain from. By working through each stakeholder's positions for each of the nine key stages, it is possible to see how their expectations at each stage are or are not being met; this, in turn, will relate to their VfM points and parameters.

Thus, for key stage 3, the public sector will be very busy trying to ensure that their needs and requirements are captured in the contract documents, that they have as many safeguards as possible in the contract to protect their interests. The contractor will be doing exactly the same thing, but from a different perspective. It is this opposing fiduciary duty as between these two parties that makes the introduction of a tracking mechanism interesting. It is possible to see that even though the main parties to this project, are pursuing the same goal, they are doing it for reasons that are often poles apart.

Financial/contract close: key stage 4

This stage is the signing of the contract and after the chinking of champagne glasses has ceased, all stakeholders at this stage of the process are able to show that there is an impact on their expectations. As the signing is taking place, it is likely that all stakeholders experience a positive move towards their expectations from the baseline measure, the baseline measure being the foundation or benchmark from where either positive or negative fluctuations can be tracked. However, as the ink dries and the stakeholders start to understand the nuances of a project, particularly as key stage 5 and works stage commence and progress, the tracking mechanism will show a rise and fall for each of the stakeholders as individual and collective expectations are achieved or otherwise.

84 *Identification of the VfM stages*

Works stage: key stage 5

Key stage 5 is the most significant stage; it is the stage where there is most risk for all of the stakeholders. The risk profile will move between each of the stakeholders as the project progresses. For example, it may well be that for the contractor the ground conditions that they were expecting are either worse than they thought (outcome a), or better than they thought (outcome b). The consequence of the actual conditions being discovered in full and resulting in an (a) or (b) position means that there has either been a negative or positive impact on the expected position. This position can then be shown on the tracking mechanism as a +ve rise or a -ve dip. As the mechanism needs to "live" the best way for this to be shown at this juncture is through the simple use of a graph, which is discussed further in the chapter. As the works stage progresses and the identified risks move across each of the stakeholders, then the risks as they move should also be tracked. This will not only allow the achievement of VfM or not to be tracked, but it will also show the trend and how the allocation of risk at any given time correlates with who is or is not achieving a VfM position at that point in the project's time. In tracking VfM regularly during this high risk period, perhaps at a monthly project board for each of the stakeholders, not only are VfM risks identified early, but early mitigation and warning strategies can then be implemented. By positioning VfM as an important feature within a risk matrix and making it an agenda item at project board, ensures that when the time comes for the critics to appear, there is at least contemporaneous evidence to show the actual position of VfM and where the risks sit at any given stage. Transparent evidence of VfM would seem to be significantly lacking at the given time (2019) and thus debates can become emotional rather than being based on factual positions. As a project heads into its handover phase is potentially when there is more of a public interest in its VfM position. Suddenly the political arm of the public sector wants to showcase its legacy or criticise its opponents for pursuing an expensive folly! In both scenarios, the information that is lacking is tangible evidence to show how VfM has been achieved; yes, there are the financial balances that can be scrutinised and cabinet project reports that can be audited to give a view of the position, but, ultimately, they do not show the full story.

Handover and defects period: key stage 6

In order to be completely effective and to align with the HMT ex post and ex ante reviews, VfM should continue to be tracked beyond the works stage; once the building has been finished, responsibilities and liabilities still sit with the stakeholders for a number of years thereafter. It may well be that the contractor achieves that utopian position of a defect-free construction. Experience dictates that this is not likely. Buildings move, weather and construction conditions often leach out of the finished project. Things sometimes go wrong. Historically, it is during this period of time that the contractor sees most of its critics. The contractor by this time has moved onto another project and therefore concentrates its resource elsewhere; defects are left not attended to. This conduct also has an impact on each stakeholder's VfM; from the contractor's perspective, this would be a negative impact as it would lead to reputational damage. From the public sector purchaser perspective there would be a negative impact, reputational damage, for not having strict contract conditions, perhaps loss of income if the facility is not being utilised to its fullest extent; and from a beneficiary perspective, perhaps being unable to utilise the development for its intended purpose. In just a normal design and build contract, this would be a disastrous situation, particularly if all stakeholder expectations weren't being achieved. However, the regular tracking of VfM, throughout the life of the project, and by all parties, should reduce the likelihood of such an outcome arising. It is sad to see that even in 2019, in the UK, many public sector design and build projects end up in this position, because there has been no monitoring of VfM. This is in spite of the fact that public sector in the UK is required by statute to comply with its best value duties as set out in the 1972 Local Government Act.

Facilities management and use of facility: key stage 7

Within key stage 6 above, the example of a design and build contract is referenced, however, VfM extends beyond that stage. The continued management, use and care of the facility also fit within this arena. If a building is not maintained, used properly or cared for, it will very quickly deteriorate. Simply getting the keys to a new building and then not doing anything with it will soon result in a dilapidated building. Thus it is imperative to maintain a tracking system to monitor this period. If this period of time is to be carried out by a third-party contractor, then the continued tracking should form part of the contract management process. Even if the facility is being managed internally, its performance and value should continue to be tracked to ensure that it is achieving the expectations of the beneficiary. Again, it is still possible within this stage to track the VfM parameters and expectations of the stakeholders who remain involved with the project.

Lifecycle and maintenance period: key stage 8

This period is one of the most criticised periods beyond that of the works stage and yet it is the area that is least managed by all stakeholders who are party to a design, build and facilities management contract. It is also arguable one of the most abused parts of the contract. Therefore, to ensure that VfM tracking continues within this period of time should be prioritised. It appears to be that this is where the most profit is made by the private sector at the expense of the public sector, and for no reason other than public sector naivety. If the VfM tracking continued in this stage as a reported mechanism, this scenario would be significantly reduced, because the

86 *Identification of the VfM stages*

opportunities for contractors to manipulate events would be identified and either managed or stopped.

Post-contract years outputs achieved: key stage 9

The final stages are of equal importance if a development or building is not achieving that output that it was expected to or responding to any new environments as expected this would have an impact on VfM. As an example, if a school, hospital or other facility were not performing as it should, then, without tangible tracking mechanisms to understand why, where and when it went wrong, it becomes more complicated to resolve and mitigate the loss.

Each of the nine key stages of a capital build project is equally important in the making of the whole. Each element should be tracked from each stakeholder's perspective and trends identified to ensure that VfM is achieved. Projects that are manged poorly tend to be the ones that perform poorly and have a negative impact on the expectations of the stakeholders and, consequently, on the ability to achieve VfM. Conversely, if a procurement process is performed properly and diligently, using tracking mechanisms can have a positive financial impact on achieving VfM.

While the tests for VfM have evolved quite significantly over the decades, it remains fairly useless unless a mechanism is adopted to track the ongoing VfM progress, not just from a public sector perspective, but also across each sector. This chapter continues to explain how each stakeholder can track its own and the collective VfM progress, simply and easily.

How to track VfM

The benefit of every stakeholder undertaking this exercise is that the tracking of the VfM progress throughout the period of a project and beyond will reveal project trends. It does not matter that, in some cases, one stakeholder may be showing a -ve position, while another is showing a +ve position; the value of the exercise is to be able to understand what is causing the trend and how that can either be mitigated or maximised depending on the result.

The purpose of setting identifiable milestones at an early stage by each stakeholder establishes a baseline of where the parties to the project expect to achieve a value for the work, time and costs dedicated to the project up to and including that point in time. Setting the milestones also assists with a collaborative understanding of where the values of a project sit for each stakeholder. This understanding and in part collaborative working, while scoffed at within the industry, can derive benefits for all. VfM can be achieved if all parties work together for the benefit of one another's goals, because as is easily identifiable some of the individual goals appear in different stakeholder lists (probably for different reasons) but if the achievement of a common goal brings about two distinct positive impacts then the outcome must be that each party has for that identified expectation achieved a VfM point.

Identification of the VfM stages 87

In setting milestones for a project examples can be keeping them realistic and aligning them to the key stage 1, feasibility or business plan, this part of the planning could also align with the Royal Institute of British Architects (RIBA) plan of works stages and sit very nicely within each RIBA stage 1 to 7; obviously the tracking mechanism would need to go beyond the RIBA stages, but; in the first instance; the tracking mechanism could work concurrently.

Year 0–1

Feasibility – commence VfM plan and initiate tracking mechanism: key stage 1

RIBA 1: Identify the business plan, expectations of stakeholders in line with the strategic case, the economic case, the commercial case, the financial case and the management position; develop the project brief, identify for the individual project the key milestones for the achievement of individual stakeholder VfM (expectations).

RIBA 2: Develop concept design and project strategies, cost information and procurement information, test the VfM tracking parameters against each stakeholder expectations for the key stage achievements.

Year 1–2

Procurement process: key stage 2

RIBA 3: Undertake procurement, undertake further design, development strategies, develop risk matrix and test the VfM tracking parameters against the stakeholder expectations. Continue with the RIBA work plan requirements, and test VfM tracking mechanism to manage and monitor trends and risks.

Preferred bidder stage and financial/contract close: key stages 3 and 4

RIBA 4: Prepare and finalise technical design, finalise construction strategy, conclude the contracts based on final documentation including any necessary novation processes and test VfM tracking mechanism to manage and monitor trends and risks

Year 2–3

Works and handover and defects period: key stages 5 and 6

RIBA 5 and 6: Construction, handover and close out.

Undertake the construction of the project, resolve design queries as they arise, administer the building contract and test VfM tracking mechanism to manage and monitor trends and risks throughout construction phase reporting any issues as they arise until such time as to achieve handover.

88 Identification of the VfM stages

Provide strategy for VfM testing to be continued throughout the handover, snagging and defects periods.

Years 3–25

Facilities management and use of facility and lifecycle and maintenance: key stages 7 and 8

RIBA 7: Undertake all in use facilities management services to align with requisite contract and ensure the continuation of the VfM tracking process to manage and monitor trends and risks, and benchmark as necessary the customer services satisfaction of the service delivery to be fed into the VfM tracking information.

Years 25–50

Post-contract outputs achieved: key stage 9

No RIBA equivalent.

The VfM tracking mechanism to be utilised at regular intervals to show how and whether the expectations of the project are being achieved from the stakeholder perspectives.

VfM tracking aims

The aim is to keep this process as simple as possible, if this is a convoluted, costly and time-consuming process it will not be used, which defeats the purpose of having the mechanism. It is envisaged that no more than one hour will be required in the preparation of the first tracking chart; once this process is completed it is expected that to update the chart for future meetings will be no more than 30 minutes and subsumed into the documents to be prepared for general reporting purposes to the relevant strategic and project boards within each of the stakeholder groups and the collective project management teams.

It is anticipated that a form of graph is the simplest method to show the flow or fluctuation of the VfM trend. The graph should set out on the horizontal axis the period in years, therefore using the identified years and stages above, the horizontal axis could be:

Yr 0–1   Yr 1–2   Yr 2–3   Yrs 3–25   Yrs 25–50
Key stage 1 KS 2, 3 4   KS 5, 6   KS 7, 8   KS 9

The vertical axis therefore needs to show either the expectation or a value to align to the expectation to demonstrate the positive and negative impact on a project that any action, inaction or project event might have on that underlying expectation. To ensure that the tracking does not begin to get complicated, it is thought that the simplest way to achieve this might be to start the vertical axis at −10 (negative 10) or less to represent not achieving VfM, such a score would indicate areas significantly falling below expectations, moving up through the axis to a baseline of 0 (zero) indicating neither the achieving of nor falling below standards, simply providing a provision, but not anticipating or expecting a VfM element at this time and finally progressing to a +10 (positive 10) to show how much above the baseline standard VfM has been achieved, with the +10 indicating significant achievement of VfM and potentially added value. Table 4.1 gives examples of the potential incidents that could cause both +ve and -ve fluctuations.

Identification of risk

Risk is a key factor in any project and tends to align with VfM: the more risk that a stakeholder carries, the less likely that stakeholder is to be achieving VfM. More often than not risk at some point within a project sits either with one party or the other. The tracking mechanism envisages that, where a party may not be achieving expectations or where within the project the value sits at 0, an element of risk is being carried by the party not achieving and having a clear understanding and being able to track that within the VfM data will be imperative in understanding the flow or fluctuation of VfM throughout the life of the project.

It is therefore expected that risk workshops that are held and where risks are identified that it is cross-referenced to the VfM tracking system at the key milestone stages. This has the benefit of identifying and managing risk strategies in the early course so that there are no surprises and so far as possible no unforeseen costs emerging. There will, however, in some circumstances be the unknown unknowns, but in going through this process even the unknown unknowns can be better managed and mitigated against with earlier interventions.

Developing the tracking mechanism

The mechanism is expected to be visual rather than a written report. The visualisation of where the project VfM peaks, flows or dips is immediate and is more of an effective discussion tool, to enable the discussions to question what the issues are that are preventing either a baseline position from being achieved or a positive score along the axis. By having the ability to see where one party is not achieving and understanding why in an open, honest and transparent arena assists in understanding how an early dip might impact on the future milestones and address issues in the early course of a project.

It is believed that by implementing this very simple tracking mechanism within regular project meetings develops a number of positive outcomes:

1 A better understanding of all the expectations.
2 A better use of collaborative and partnership working.

90 *Identification of the VfM stages*

3 An early warning system in the event of unforeseen risks giving rise to early interventions and mitigation.
4 Better risk management.
5 Achievement of VfM on the concluded project by all stakeholders.

The next section of this chapter takes a snapshot look at some of the standard form commercial contracts that are used in construction and engineering projects. This is being undertaken to allow both academia and practitioners, who might not otherwise know, how the industry deals with VfM. This also enables the final chapter to discuss the contractual provisions that should be implemented going forward to encapsulate the tracking mechanism and to ensure that it is utilised appropriately by the parties.

A review of the mechanisms currently encapsulated in contract documents

The analysis of many standard form contract documents identifies that there is no mechanism to require project participants or others to proactively track the achievement of VfM, which considering the importance that is placed on its achievement seems to be an anomaly that is very easy to address. In order to further test this position, the major construction and engineering standard form contracts have been scrutinised to find what level of importance they place on VfM; it transpired that the major standard form contracts do not place any importance on the concept at all. The first contract searched was the JCT Design and Build Contract 2016. This contract was selected as the main contract used in construction, currently by local authorities and other public sector bodies. There is in fact no mention at all of VfM, either in terms of achieving it or of tracking it; the need to achieve best value, by a process of benchmarking or achieving key performance indicators is, however, mentioned, in the JCT Service Agreement developed for use by the public sector and rather than this clause being a fundamental requirement of the agreement, it is actually identified as being an optional element. Indeed, even the optional, non-binding partnering charter only suggests that there should be an ethos of adding value. On this basis, it would appear that this suite of standard form contracts does not seek to require the achievement of VfM.

Turning now to the competitor suite of contracts, the NEC, which has been strongly promoted by the UK central government departments as the best form of contract to use to generate a partnering, collaborative working project, it can be seen that, while the focus is more on collaborative working, with each party being required to "work in the spirit of mutual trust and confidence", again there is no requirement to achieve VfM or to track it.

By reviewing the two major suites of standard form contracts, both of which are used not only in the UK but also internationally, it is evident that while a great deal of importance is put on achieving VfM, it is only truly a lip service provision.

Table 4.1 Identification of stakeholder group VfM value and fluctuations at each key stage

	Central government	Local government (procuring entity)	Contractor	Financier		Beneficiary	
				Debt	Equity	Employee	End user
Feasibility	Enabling work determines whether project can proceed Starting point 0 value	Enabling work determines whether project can proceed Starting point 0 value	Enabling work determines whether project can proceed Starting point 0 value	No involvement 0 value	No involvement 0 value	Minimal involvement 0 value	Minimal involvement 0 value
Procurement	Progressing development Teasing out best solution, best contractor ascertain market solutions Value rising but not significant, highlights competitive market and potential for a good deal Cost and resource commitment	Cost and resource commitment Progressing development Teasing out best solution, best contractor ascertain market solutions Value rising but not significant, highlights competitive market and potential for a good deal	Negotiation process Risk Cost Competition Resource Time Opportunity to bid Experience development Kudos Reputation Business development 0 value or rising −ve and +ve drivers are here but risk and cost probability of success ratio should be considered could be −ve value	Little involvement with contractor on notice but not committed small value rising from 0	Involvement limited finance ringfenced therefore potential −ve score based on the fact that the ringfenced resource is no longer available and not being used	0 value little or limited involvement potential −ve impact on resource and time dealing with contractor questions rising to +ve with knowledge that a new facility and resource is being progressed	0 value, end user still in old facility and has no benefit at this stage

	Central government	Local government (procuring entity)	Contractor	Financier		Beneficiary	
Preferred bidder		Deal almost achieved Increase in value reputation, kudos, positive solutions	Preferred bidder Losing contractor –ve value Winning contractor +ve value increasing Risk, cost and time factors still to be considered	Increased activity and increased value rates and commercial bankability being addressed therefore value increasing quickly	Increased activity value raising as ringfenced money to be utilised	0 value, end user still in old facility and has no benefit at this stage	0 value, end user still in old facility and has no benefit at this stage
Financial close	Deal achieved HMT sign off of commercial deal rising value and release promissory note in relation to the PFI contribution	Deal achieved Kudos, start on site Policy and targets commenced Reputation community engagement	Contract agreed Rise in value but not high rise Minimal value accruing Procurement risk lessened Still at high risk stage	SWAP rates interest agreed for fixed rate over 25years Contract conditions agreed and entered all rights protected Low risk deal High value – base line value achieved	Increased activity value raising as ringfenced money to be utilised	0 value, end user still in old facility and has no benefit at this stage	0 value, end user still in old facility and has no benefit at this stage

	Central government	Local government (procuring entity)	Contractor	Financier		Beneficiary	
Construction period	Minimal rise in value, asset being developed risk in project lowers PFI funding still sitting with gov. dept. not released until service availability and then drawn down on a month-by-month basis through holding company	Risk but no cost Construction and programme monitoring and dealing with matters arising Value increasing assuming a good project has potential to swing to –ve if bad deal agreed	High risk, cost, reputation, time, drawdown of debt no income generation from contracting authority until service availability	-ve value, debt serviced repayment profile to be adhered to but initial drawdown at a loss	Rise in value equity provision into a tangible asset as construction progresses	0 value, end user still in old facility and has no benefit at this stage	0 value, end user still in old facility and has no benefit at this stage
Service availability	High rise to value achieved, stop using old building start to use new facilities	High rise to value achieved, stop using old building start to use new facilities and community to derive the benefit Payments to be made and maintained and strong contract management required	High rise to value achieved, completion of build contract, risk of construction disappears Payment profile from contracting authority commences Profit margins can now be realised DLP and snags outstanding	High rise to value achieved, stop using old building start to use new facilities	High rise to value achieved, stop using old building start to use new facilities	High rise to value achieved, stop using old building start to use new facilities; new technology and innovative sustainable buildings	High rise to value achieved, stop using old building start to use new facilities Service tested by willingness to pay and willingness to use

	Central government	Local government (procuring entity)	Contractor	Financier	Beneficiary	
Operation period	Maintain position along a base line value situation neither improves nor declines	Contract performance working and continual improvement targets being maintained value rises incrementally until handback Alternatively, value maintains a position along the baseline because contractual terms and expectations are being achieved Strong contract management required	Facilities management to maintain and perform in accordance with contract provisions Programmed maintenance, technology refresh Achieve deliverable targets without deductions being levied Value continues to rise	Maintain position along a base line value situation neither improves nor declines Until a point of refinancing and then a peak into higher value than baseline position	High rise to value achieved, stop using old building start to use new facilities; new technology and innovative sustainable buildings	Value maintained at high level of community benefit
Repayment period			Facilities management to maintain and perform in accordance with contract provisions Programmed maintenance, technology refresh Achieve deliverable targets without deductions being levied Value continues to rise	Payment profile maintained starting to peak as investment profit reached	High rise to value achieved, stop using old building start to use new facilities; new technology and innovative sustainable buildings	Value maintained at high level of community benefit

	Central government	Local government (procuring entity)	Contractor	Financier		Beneficiary	
Year 25–50			No further involvement with the exception perhaps of any DLP to any recent works or warranty provisions Value decreases to 0	Repayments made Profit achieved No further value in project unless refinanced Drops to 0 value		High rise to value achieved, stop using old building start to use new facilities; new technology and innovative sustainable buildings	Value maintained at high level of community benefit
Year 26–50	Tangible asset on public sector balance sheet with a value and further life provision Depending on policy at this time future availability of finance	Tangible asset on public sector balance sheet with a value and further life provision Depending on policy at this time future availability of finance	No further involvement Value decreases to 0	No further involvement 0 value		Value maintained at high level of employee benefit Potential to decline during this period relative to policy and availability of money to maintain to operations standards	Value maintained at high level of community benefit Potential to decline during this period relative to policy and availability of money to maintain to operations standards

Works cited

Liu, J., Love, P., Davis, P., Smith, J. & Regan, M. (2013). Performance Measurement Framework in PPP Projects. *PPP International Body of Knowledge*. Preston: University of Central Lancashire Press.

Neely, A., Gregory, M. & Platts, K. (2005). Performance Measurement System Design: a Literature Review and Research Agenda. *International Journal of Operations and Management*, 1228–1263.

5 The need for the VfM tracking mechanism

How to track VfM

The benefit of every stakeholder undertaking this exercise is that the tracking of VfM progress, throughout the period of a project and beyond, will reveal project trends. It does not matter that, in some cases, one stakeholder may be showing a -ve position, while another is showing a +ve position, the value of the exercise is to be able to understand what is causing the trend and how that can either be mitigated or maximised depending on the result.

The purpose of setting identifiable milestones at an early stage by each stakeholder establishes a baseline of where the parties to the project expect to achieve a value whether that is financial or otherwise, which meets their incentives and drivers, for undertaking the project, for the work, time and costs dedicated up to and including that point in time. Setting the milestones also assists with a collaborative understanding of where the values of a project sit for each stakeholder. This understanding and, in part, collaborative working, while scoffed at within the industry, can drive benefits for all. VfM can be achieved if all parties work together for the benefit of one another's goals, because, as is easily identifiable, some of the individual goals appear in different stakeholder lists (probably for different reasons) but if the achievement of a common goal brings about distinct positive impacts, then the outcome must be that each party has for that identified expectation achieved a VfM point.

In setting milestones for a project examples can be keeping them realistic and aligning them to the key stage 1, feasibility or business plan, this part of the planning could also align with the Royal Institute of British Architects (RIBA) plan of works stages and sit very nicely within each RIBA stage 1 to 7; obviously the tracking mechanism would need to go beyond the RIBA stages, but, in the first instance, the tracking mechanism could work concurrently.

Year 0–1 Feasibility – commence VfM plan and initiate tracking mechanism: key stage 1

RIBA 1: Identify the business plan, expectations of stakeholders in line with the strategic case, the economic case, the commercial case, the financial case and

98 *The need for the VfM tracking mechanism*

the management position; develop the project brief, identify for the individual project the key milestones for the achievement of individual stakeholder VfM (expectations).

RIBA 2: Develop concept design, and project strategies, cost information and procurement information, test the VfM tracking parameters against each stakeholder's expectations for the key stage achievements.

Year 1–2

Procurement process: key stage 2

RIBA 3: Undertake procurement, undertake further design, development strategies, develop risk matrix and test the VfM tracking parameters against stakeholder expectations. Continue with the RIBA work plan requirements and test VfM tracking mechanism to manage and monitor trends and risks.

Preferred bidder stage and financial/contract close: key stages 3 and 4

RIBA 4: Prepare and finalise technical design, finalise construction strategy, conclude the contracts based on final documentation including any necessary novation processes, and test VfM tracking mechanism to manage and monitor trends and risks.

Year 2–3

Works and handover and defects period: key stages 5 and 6

RIBA 5 and 6: Construction, handover and close out.

Undertake the construction of the project, resolve design queries as they arise, administer the building contract and test VfM tracking mechanism to manage and monitor trends and risks throughout construction phase reporting any issues as they arise until such time as to achieve handover. Provide strategy for VfM testing to be continued throughout the handover, snagging and defects periods.

Years 3–25

Facilities management and use of facility and lifecycle and maintenance: key stages 7 and 8

RIBA 7: Undertake all in use, facilities management services to align with requisite contract and ensure the continuation of the VfM tracking process to manage and monitor trends and risks, and benchmark as necessary the customer services satisfaction of the service delivery to be fed into the VfM tracking information.

The need for the VfM tracking mechanism 99

Years 25–50

Post-contract outputs achieved: key stage 9

No RIBA equivalent.

The VfM tracking mechanism to be utilised at regular intervals to show how and whether the expectations of the project are being achieved from stakeholder perspectives.

VfM tracking aims

The aim is to keep this process as simple as possible; if this is a convoluted, costly and time-consuming process it will not be used, which defeats the purpose of having the mechanism. It is envisaged that no more than one hour will be required in the preparation of the first tracking chart; once this process is completed it is expected that to update the chart for future meetings will be no more than 30 minutes and subsumed into the documents to be prepared for general reporting purposes to the relevant strategic and project boards within each of the stakeholder groups and the collective project management teams.

It is anticipated that a form of graph is the simplest method to show the flow or fluctuation of the VfM trend. The graph should set out on the horizontal axis the period in years, therefore using the identified years and stages above, the horizontal axis could be:

Yr 0–1	Yr 1–2	Yr 2–3	Yrs 3–25	Yrs 25–50
Key stage 1	KS 2, 3, 4	KS 5, 6	KS 7, 8	KS 9

The vertical axis therefore needs to show either the expectation or a value to align to the expectation to demonstrate the positive and negative impact on a project that any action, inaction, or project event might have upon that underlying expectation. To ensure that the tracking does not begin to get complicated, it is thought that the simplest way to achieve this might be to start the vertical axis at −10 (negative 10) or less to represent not achieving VfM, such a score would indicate areas significantly falling below expectations, moving up through the axis to a baseline of 0 (zero) indicating neither the achieving of nor falling below standards, simply providing a provision, but not anticipating or expecting a VfM element at this time and finally progressing to a +10 (positive 10) to show how much above the baseline standard VfM has been achieved, with the +10 indicating significant achievement of VfM and potentially added value. Table 5.1 gives examples of the potential incidents that could cause both −ve and -ve fluctuations.

Table 5.1 Identification of stakeholder VfM tracking values

Table 5.1 **Identification of stakeholder VfM tracking values**

Stake holder / Stage	Central government (gatekeeper)	Local government (procuring entity)	Contractor	Financier		Beneficiary	
				Debt	Equity	Debtpurchaser or end user of services	Equityowner of building
Feasibility: starting point	• Determining whether project can proceed • Implementation of system of reviews	• Determining whether project can proceed • Developing business plan, vision and budgets • Committing resource (a cost without any tangible benefit to be had as yet)	• Contractor feasibility costing and scoping the project	• Assessing rates of return	• Assessing rates of return	• Consultees	• Consultees
	• 0 value	• -ve value	• 0 value	• 0 value	• 0 value	• 0 value	• 0 value

Stake holder Stage	Central government (gatekeeper)	Local government (procuring entity)	Contractor	Financier		Beneficiary	
				Debt	Equity	Debtpurchaser or end user of services	Equityowner of building
Procurement:planning,market engagement, contractor bidding and tender evaluation	• Manging reviews and advising as necessary • Budget planning and compliance checking • Final approvals	• Planning procurement solution • Developing bid documents scoring criteria and contract documents • Undertaking all steps necessary to formally engage with market • Contractor procurement and evaluation • Selection of bidder	• Establish risk of project, cost, resource and time in value for the company in progressing the project to determine if it is in the company's interests to join the competition • Engage in the procurement process in competition with other contractors • Submit final bid; await evaluation outcome	• Limited involvement with contractor (s) but not fully committed	• Limited Involvement • Finance ringfenced (–ve score based on the fact that the ringfenced resource is no longer available and not being used)	• Limited involvement • Impact on resources through stakeholder engagement • Time dealing with contractor questions • End user still in old facility and has no benefit at this stage	• End user still in old facility and has no benefit at this stage
	0 value	0 value	-ve value	0 value	-ve value	-ve value	0 value

Stake holder / Stage	Central government (gatekeeper)	Local government (procuring entity)	Contractor	Financier		Beneficiary	
				Debt	Equity	Debtpurchaser or end user of services	Equityowner of building
Preferred bidder	• Execution of any necessary documents	• Confirmation and clarification of preferred bidder • Contract Award	• Preferred Bidder status achieved • Confirmation and clarification of outstanding issues • Contract award	• Increased activity as the deal is settled • Commercial bankability being addressed, and final documents agreed	• Increased activity • Ringfenced money to be utilised	• End user still in old facility and has no benefit at this stage • Resource commitment in dealing with preferred bidder and planning for works; potential relocation and disruption to service	• Old facility still being used and costs associated with keeping a dilapidated building going for a period of time until new facility available
	+ve value	+ ve value	+ve value but not rising to 0 value (risk of judicial review period, challenge of procurement, start on site high level of contractor risk)	+ ve value above the 0 base rate as the deal is sealed	+ve value	-ve value	-ve value

Stake holder / Stage	Central government (gatekeeper)	Local government (procuring entity)	Contractor	Financier		Beneficiary	
				Debt	Equity	Debt purchaser or end user of services	Equity/owner of building
Financial close	• Deal achieved • Parliamentary sign off of commercial deal • Release promissory note in relation to PFI contribution or other project funding as agreed + ve value	• Deal achieved • Policy and targets being realised • Reputation among stakeholders and community being maintained + ve value	• Contract agreed • Mobilisation details of project put in place • Procurement risk lessened • Still at high risk stage +ve increase in value above 0	• SWAP rates interest agreed for fixed rate over 25 years • Contract conditions agreed and entered all rights protected • Low risk deal – high value return +ve value	• Increased activity value raising as ring-fenced money to be utilised • Profit likely • Low risk deal – high value return +ve value	• End user still in old facility and has no benefit at this stage • Resource commitment dealing with preferred bidder and planning for works; relocation and disruption to service -ve value	• No change from the above -ve value

Stake holder Stage	Central government (gatekeeper)	Local government (procuring entity)	Contractor	Financier		Beneficiary	
				Debt	Equity	Debtpurchaser or end user of services	Equityowner of building
Construction period	• Realisation of a new asset to support political aspirations and targets	• Risk but no cost • Construction and programme monitoring • Dealing with matters arising • Reputational position and political will	• High risk, cost, commitment and reputational impact, in terms of programme and achieving affordability targets • Type of project depends on flow of income	• Debt serviced repayment profile to be adhered to, but initial drawdown at a loss	• Equity provision into a tangible asset as construction progresses	• No change from the above	• No change from the above
	+ve value	+ ve value assuming a good project has potential to swing to −ve if bad deal agreed	+ve if risk is as expected	-ve value	+ve value	-ve value	-ve value

Stake holder Stage	Central government (gatekeeper)	Local government (procuring entity)	Contractor	Financier		Beneficiary	
				Debt	Equity	Debtpurchaser or end user of services	Equityowner of building
Service availability	• If achieved on time and on budget, new asset and political reputation increases	• Start to use new facilities and potential to realise capital asset from sale of old building • Community to derive the benefits • Payments to be made and maintained • Fewer maintenance costs • Longer life span of building • Strong contract management required • Potential increase in income generation	• Completion of build contract • Risks during the construction period disappears • Payment profile from contracting authority commences • Profit margins can now be realised • Defects liability period and snags outstanding	• Repayments are being made and maintained • No risk of step into project • Potential realisation of profit	• Repayments commence • No risk of step in	• Stop using old building with a potential capital gain if sold • Start to use new facilities • New technology and user experience lifted • User requirements met	• Stop using old building • Start to use new facilities • Service tested by willingness to pay and willingness to use by end user reflected in pricing and ability to profit
	+ve value	+ve value	+ve value	+ve value	+ve value	+ ve value	+ve value

Stake holder Stage	Central government (gatekeeper)	Local government (procuring entity)	Contractor	Financier		Beneficiary	
				Debt	Equity	Debtpurchaser or end user of services	Equityowner of building
Operation period	Maintain position if contract outputs being achieved	• Continual improvement • Targets being maintained • Added value being undertaken	• Facilities management to maintain and perform in accordance to contract provisions • Programmed maintenance, technology refresh • Achieve deliverable targets without deductions being levied	• Maintain position along a base line • Value situation neither improves nor declines • Until a point of refinancing and then a peak into higher value than baseline position	Repayments continue	• Continued use of new building, community benefit being achieved	• Socio-economic impact tangible with achievement of expectations in outputs
	+ve base line value	+ve increases, baseline maintenance or -ve decreases depending on service provided	+ ve value	+ve peak above expectation achievement if refinance takes place	= maintenance of a baseline position	+ve value	+ve value

Stake holder Stage	Central government (gatekeeper)	Local government (procuring entity)	Contractor	Financier		Beneficiary	
				Debt	Equity	Debtpurchaser or end user of services	Equityowner of building
Repayment period	As above	As above, unless disputes or poor service become apparent and not rectified	• Facilities management to maintain and perform in accordance to contract provisions • Programmed maintenance, technology refresh • Achieve deliverable targets without deductions being levied • Value continues to rise unless deductions are being levied and contractual issues for poor services are being implemented	• Payment profile maintained starting to peak as investment profit reached		• High rise in value achieved • Stop using old building • Start to use new facilities • New technology and innovative sustainable buildings	• Value maintained at high level of community benefit
	= value	+, -, = values applicable	-ve value applied				

Stake holder / Stage	Central government (gatekeeper)	Local government (procuring entity)	Contractor	Financier		Beneficiary	
				Debt	Equity	Debtpurchaser or end user of services	Equityowner of building
Year 25			• No further involvement with the exception perhaps of any defects liability periods to any recent works or warranty provisions	• Repayments made • Profit achieved • No further value in project unless refinanced		• Use of a building which has gone back to public ownership • Available funding may decrease the maintenance • May decrease the level of service provision Policy and political constraints on service may have an impact	• Value maintained at high level of community benefit • Or building to suffer budget constraints
			0 value	0 value		+ve and -ve implications at this time	+ve and -ve outcome likely

Stake holder / Stage	Central government (gatekeeper)	Local government (procuring entity)	Contractor	Financier		Beneficiary	
				Debt	Equity	Debtpurchaser or end user of services	Equityowner of building
Year 26–50	• Tangible asset on public sector balance sheet with a value and further life provision • Depending on policy at this time, future availability of finance	• Tangible asset on public sector balance sheet with a value and further life provision • Depending on policy at this time, future availability of finance	• No further involvement	• No further involvement	No further involvement	• Potential for both the service and the fabric of the building to decline during these years depending on policy and availability of money to maintain to operation al standards • End user seek alternative provision from private sector	• Maintenance liability reduced funding and reduced user needs (depending on facility and government policy both locally and nationally)
	+ve and -ve impact	+ve and -ve impact	0 value	0 value	0 value	-ve value	-ve value

Developing the tracking mechanism

The mechanism is expected to be visual rather than a written report. The visualisation of where the project VfM peaks, flows or dips is immediate and is more of an effective discussion tool to enable questioning of what the issues are which are preventing either a baseline position from being achieved or a positive score along the axis. By having the ability to see where one party is not achieving and understanding why in an open, honest and transparent arena assists in understanding how an early dip might impact on the future milestones and address issues in the early course of a project.

It is believed that by implementing this very simple tracking mechanism within regular project meetings develops a number of positive outcomes:

1 A better understanding of all the expectations.
2 A better use of collaborative and partnership working.
3 An early warning system in the event of unforeseen risks giving rise to early interventions and mitigation.
4 Better risk management.
5 Achievement of VfM on the concluded project by all stakeholders.

Table 5.1 identifies for each stakeholder group a form of valuation of where the VfM point can be tracked. Thus a zero (0) balance could be the baseline starting point. No expectations are anticipated, no working is being carried out – potentially, this would be at the point where the feasibility planning or business case preparation is being carried out, as, at that point no one knows whether a project is going to go ahead or whether it is merely a fact-finding exercise.

The concept drawings for each stakeholder group highlighting how this should work and be utilised to develop the findings are set out below.

In order to further advance these concept drawings, a method of identifying the stakeholder group VfM points was required. Year 0 was identified as being the starting point and at which time it was considered that there could potentially be a -ve value on the tracking mechanism; this was to reflect the fact that at this stage the only stakeholders involved would be the public sector and the potential beneficiaries. The public sector stakeholders would at this stage of the process, Year 0, be undertaking a number of steps. These steps would include their initial or outline submission to central government for consideration depending on the individual country's processes and depending on the type of project or contract being procured and the form of funding or investment needed.

The beneficiaries would also be in a -ve position, as they are not deriving the full benefit of a building or facilities that are fit for purpose. While it can be argued that the feasibility stage for each stakeholder group does not take place at the same time, in fact, each stakeholder (except the beneficiary) will at the commencement of a project undertake a business case strategy before undertaking a project, to determine if it is worth pursuing. On the basis of

The need for the VfM tracking mechanism 111

the foregoing, it seems both reasonable and logical that this should be a starting point and that either a 0 value or a -ve value be attached, since, at this stage, the undertaking of the feasibility process is not giving a benefit or generating a profit, perhaps the current building or service provision is a -ve cost against budgets aligning with the -ve considerations, this starting parameter could be determined by the parties individually or collectively.

Having given thought to the starting process and stage 1, each of the key stages was considered and at each stage thought was given as to the impact on each of the stakeholder groups and a value attached as identified in Table 5.1. Stage 2, being the procurement process, up to the preferred bidder stage and financial close, these areas were again considered to warrant a -ve value, particularly for the private sector contractors, who may not achieve preferred bidder. This rationale is supported as the procurement process has undergone a significant amount of criticism for allowing time overruns and procuring entities not carrying out processes efficiently. The link to the stakeholder group milestones also supports the position that this key stage of the procurement process does not achieve any of the +ve incentives identified by any of the stakeholder groups discussed in the previous chapter, at least not until the achievement of financial close when the stakeholder groups can start to progress the actual project.

The next seven key stages begin to link to +ve actions with the achievement of the aims and incentives and expectations identified within each of the stages and, therefore, VfM. As the project develops and as each aim becomes a reality, the gradual rise in +ve VfM considerations becomes obvious.

The concept of the tracking mechanism in the exemplars set out in the following graphs for each stakeholder group; the trend shown is based on the supposition that the project being undertaken is succeeding, at every stage, obviously, in some project procurements, there will be trends that identify a failing project. The tracking mechanism is intended to show all possible outcomes. It is for this reason that using a tracking mechanism, at each of the key stages, could be seen to be an important feature within the project management structures and the ongoing monitoring of VfM. If VfM is not being achieved at any of the key stages as expected, early discussions can be held to rectify the problem for the stakeholder groups. Establishing the values along the vertical axis to reflect the VfM points, has not been undertaken as a scientific measure, rather −10 was deemed to be an easy value to work with, as it allows a sufficiently wide enough parameter to encapsulate a divergence of below par VfM positions. Thus a woefully inadequate position, which might have resulted in contract termination, high value costs and damages, at the extreme end of a scale, to the other end of the scale, of just not quite achieved standard, could result in achieving it with amendments to practices or behaviours. A value of 0 was given to the baseline measurement, at which point it could be said that everyone was maintaining the status quo and just doing their job and, finally, from 0 to +10 being a wide enough divergence to measure the parameters, from just

112 *The need for the VfM tracking mechanism*

doing slightly more that performing the contractual position, to going those few extra miles and delivering additionality. Having developed the concept or trend graphs for the tracking mechanism, they are set out below. The details for each were gathered from an especially organised workshop attended by each of the sector specific stakeholders.

Figure 5.1 represents the senior debt funder for a design, build, finance and operate capital infrastructure deal. This shows that in the early key stages of the project, the debt funder has no expectations or incentive to be involved in a project. The interest from the debt funder begins to rise during the preferred bidder process and achieves expectations at the financial close of a project. These expectations are maintained throughout the contractual period, based on a contract that is performing in accordance with the contract terms. This trend correlates with the expectations of the bank that it would be paid on time and at a consistent rate throughout the period of finance. You would expect troughs in this if the debt was not being paid in accordance with the contract terms.

Figure 5.2 relates to the VfM point of the senior debt funders, in cases where refinance is possible. This graph represents the VfM point when the finance and project contracts are being managed very well and the project is deemed to be a strong project, at which point the financiers would then determine that the deal could be capable of being refinanced. The local authority must be in accordance with the contractual provisions to agree refinancing. The interesting point in this trend graph is that while the refinancing of a project is anticipated perhaps within some contracts, the finance stakeholder group see this as an added value to the financial deal. Arguably there are many variables, which would impact on a refinancing position. Refinancing only takes place where the project is a strong project. The

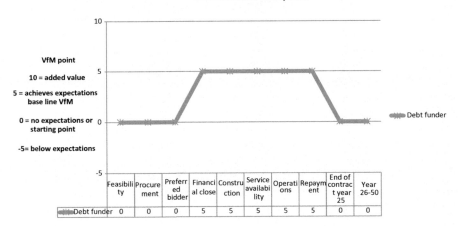

Figure 5.1 Senior debt funder

The need for the VfM tracking mechanism 113

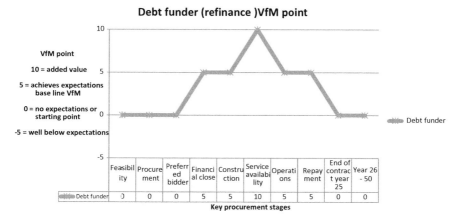

Figure 5.2 Senior debt funder

concept drawing did not originally take refinancing into consideration. There were additional discussions held by the stakeholder groups that provided additional insight into how the tracking mechanism would flow.

Figure 5.3 represents the VfM point of the equity funders, the graph they developed highlights that, in practice, at the commencement of the procurement process, during the feasibility stage up to financial close that they perceive this to be a part of the process from which they have below expectations. This is stated to be because they are pulling together their consortia and incurring costs using resources when there is no real understanding of whether the project team they are with will achieve the preferred bidder status. It is only at the preferred bidder stage and then at financial

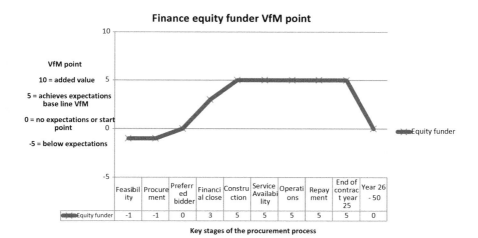

Figure 5.3 Equity funder

114 The need for the VfM tracking mechanism

close that this stakeholder group believes that it is beginning to achieve its expectations or incentives. The position of achieved expectations is maintained throughout the period of the PFI contract.

Figure 5.4 represents the construction contractor's perception of where, within the identified key stages, their VfM point was. Interestingly, the result was that they only determined that they achieved their baseline point at service availability, being the point of the contract in which they have completed their part and are ready to leave the site. The trend line then shows a rapid decline from that point. This was stated to be because they no longer had an involvement on the site but for snagging issues and the defects liability period. Further contractor information would be helpful in this area to determine the instances where contractors do provide additionality into projects and how the tracking mechanism impacts on the occurrences of such events.

Figure 5.5 represents the operations period of the contract, from service availability by the facilities management (FM) contractor. This shows that the FM perception is that from financial close until the end of the operations period the FM contractor only ever achieves expectations. The rationale presented for this position is that the contractual obligations require the FM contractor to proactively, continually improve its service provision. On that basis, the continuous improvement, which might otherwise appear to be additionality, is only deemed to be maintaining the contractual position and achieving expectations. Not unlike the construction contractor, therefore, additional and continued data as the tracking mechanism is rolled out might provide information about whether the contractual terms enhance performance or fetter performance towards achieving VfM and whether the use of the tracking mechanism would have a +ve or a −ve consequence.

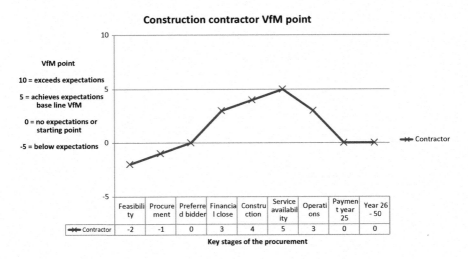

Figure 5.4 Construction contractor

The need for the VfM tracking mechanism 115

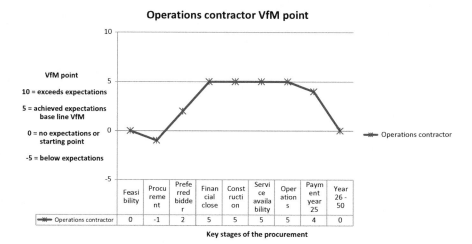

Figure 5.5 FM contractor

Figure 5.6 represents the beneficiary group. The beneficiaries held an interesting view on where they perceived their VfM expectations to be and where they achieved additionality. The view taken and presented was that, throughout the operations period, they would achieve expectations and nothing more. The surprise was that they perceived they would achieve a period of additionality just after the operations period had ended at Year 25, when they would no longer be paying for the contract. However, that brief period of additionality declined quite rapidly from Year 26 to Year 50. The reasons given for this were that they perceived that, once the public sector was back in control of operations, the decline in budgets would mean that

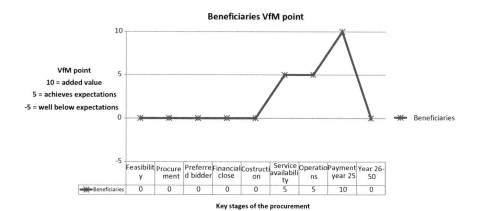

Figure 5.6 The beneficiary group

116 *The need for the VfM tracking mechanism*

the public sector would not be able to continue to maintain the asset and that, in some circumstances, the asset would become obsolete.

Figure 5.7 represents the local government stakeholder group. The local government opinion differed from the original concept drawing. It did not at any point perceive that it was in a -ve value position. It also perceived that from the service availability period it was achieving a position that was giving it slightly better value than just a base case position. It also reflected the views of the beneficiaries from Year 25 onwards. The view held was that there would be a reduction in performance standards once the contractor had gone offsite. This would be as a result of diminished budgets and a lack of personnel left within the authority to pick up roles that had been undertaken for a prolonged period of time by a contractor. The scenario presented within the discussion was that the asset could also be deemed to be obsolete from a technological perspective. The debate highlighted that there may be occasions on which the best solution for the authority might well be simply to do nothing with the building, leaving it in a state of being "mothballed".

Figure 5.8 represents central government as the contracting authority. This figure highlights that the perception from central government acting within its PF2 capacity as contracting authority. The only time that it perceives that it is achieving its baseline VfM point is from the end of the construction period to the end of Year 25 and while it has to asset on its register, the asset at the end of Year 25 will fall back to the local authority to maintain. The trend depicted within this graph correlates with the perceived position within the concept drawing.

Figure 5.9 represents an overlay of all of the stakeholder group positions to allow a visual analysis to be undertaken. This graph highlights some interesting features from the stakeholder group's perceptions. The results appear to

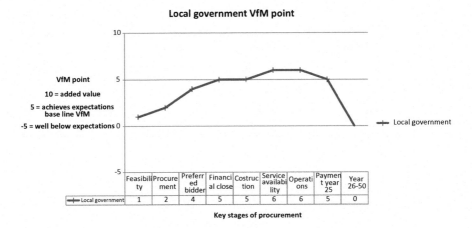

Figure 5.7 Local government

The need for the VfM tracking mechanism 117

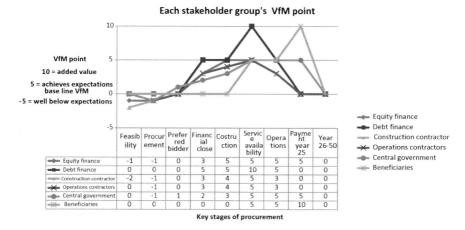

Figure 5.8 Central government

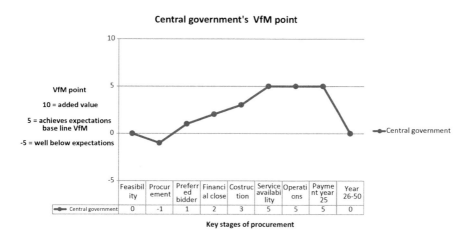

Figure 5.9 Comparison of all stakeholder groups

show that only the debt funders and the beneficiaries believe that they achieve a position where they have additionality from a project in the normal course of a project. Significantly, the trend lines for all stakeholders show a gradual incline during the feasibility and procurement phases to achieving a baseline VfM point from financial close to the end of Year 25. The differences being that the beneficiaries do not think that they have any expectations during the early stages and their trend line only increases at the point of service availability. The results portrayed are not unexpected in the main. The graph does, however, evidence that the achievement of VfM can be tracked at key stages and can be used as a quick and effective tool to

118 *The need for the VfM tracking mechanism*

determine visually where each stakeholder group is at any given time in the achievement of VfM.

Summary

This chapter set out to advance ideas proposed in Chapters 3 and 4, by exploring and developing how a VfM tracking and or testing mechanism, the Equilibrium Testing Mechanism (ETM), can work. The use of an ETM within projects could be a valuable additional tool to assist all parties achieve their aims. The main problem, however, in entrenching this into the industry is that, for it to work effectively, it needs to be rolled out not as an optional mechanism, but rather as a contractual requirement that highlights that achieving VfM is not at just a one-off, single-point-in-time exercise, it is something that can only be achieved by monitoring progress on an ongoing basis and understanding that VfM is a moving target during the course of any project, within the over the discrete key stages.

The advantage of tracking VfM, in this way is that, if one of the identified stakeholders is failing in one section in the early course of the programme, mitigations can be undertaken perhaps earlier than normal, to ensure that the risk to VfM is contained and caught up and other expectations can be managed at each of the stages to the project. In reacting this way, we can prevent the problem becoming a greater problem later in the project. Each party within the normal provisions of a contract is required to mitigate risk factors, but this tracking mechanism would allow a further layer of transparency to the project and, as a consequence of that, would assist in managing expectations overall. The benefits of including such a mechanism within the contract documents as an additional toolkit far outweighs the current lack of any mechanism to undertake such an exercise.

6 Value for money protocol, bid document and contract drafting

Final word

While there is a reluctance within the industry for this to become a contractual compliance provision, for fear that non-compliance would equate to a breach of contract, triggering penalties and ultimate termination if it is not contractual, there is little hope of such a system being implemented and effectively utilised. By implementing this tracking mechanism into UK and other international standard form contract documents, with responsibilities and obligations sitting with all parties jointly and severally, based on a collective responsibility, then it would be a difficulty for any party to trigger a termination or compensation event. Indeed, the mechanism is meant to be a tool to assist, but a tool that *must* be used, not as a discretionary option. As we have seen throughout this book, VfM fluctuates, shifting from one stakeholder to another, depending in part where the element of risk in the project is and back again throughout the different stages of any development or build contract.

Thus it is suggested that, in the first instance, bidders for projects should be required to respond on VfM within the originating bid submissions. This first exercise would be the start of identifying the incentives, drivers and expectations. Thereafter throughout the bid process, this baseline information could be developed to generate the key stages and the parameters for the vertical axis. User guidance should be adapted for each stakeholder and the tables associated with Chapters 3, 4, 5 and 6 will assist in this process. From that point onwards, the developed positions at that stage could quite simply sit within any form of contract document.

Indeed, in order to progress the mechanism, the industry institutions could support the process and consider including it within stakeholder specific contract publications. The Construction Industry Council (CIC) is already progressing an initiative to achieve this aim, the Chartered Institute of Builders (CIOB) and the Royal Institute of Chartered Surveyors (RICS), both in the UK and in an international forum, could also jointly advocate the use of the mechanism to ensure that the standard form contracts used both in the UK and within the international arena are amended to include the process.

As we have already seen, the Joint Contracts Tribunal (JCT), New Engineering Contract (NEC) and the International Federation of Consulting Engineers (FIDIC), otherwise known as Federation Internationale Des Ingénieurs-Conseils,

120   *VfM protocol and other documents*

do not incorporate any form of drafting currently that deals with the VfM point and to reiterate a statement from an earlier chapter, this is surprising, considering how important VfM is and how often it is used as a tool to decry projects. This then has an impact on reputation, not only on the public sector, but also on the private sector contractor. One would anticipate that someone would want to protect reputational standing in this regard.

While it can be seen that more openness would be needed and a transparency of dealings required on a project-by-project basis by all stakeholders, this can be no bad thing. Indeed, transparency of dealings is one of the main instruments utilised to combat corruption in a worldwide arena.

The proposed specimen document, or questionnaire, could be used as part of the bidding process, working on questions to drill down into the drivers, incentives and expectations of the contractor, for each of the key stages.

Stakeholder Group [BUILDING CONTRACTOR]	Bid Questions – VfM
Key Stage 1-	
Feasibility Stage to Procurement Process	As a contractor you will no doubt have carried out a business case or project analysis in relation to bidding for this project.
	Please confirm what your expectations are, from your own company's perspective, in relation to engaging in this process from the time that you began the feasibility stage continuing through to the procurement phase?
	Please identify how you achieve VfM in carrying out this process and all of the inherent internal risks your company faces in relation to this project only?
Key Stage 2-	
The Procurement Process to Contract Execution	Please identify your expectations from this key stage process, and how in meeting those expectations you will achieve VfM in carrying out this process incorporating all of the risks associated with meeting those expectations?
Key Stage 3-	
And so on until the table covers Key Stage 8 or 9 depending upon the identified key stages for each project specific table.	Link the same form of question to each key stage and project phase to ensure that all relevant expectations are identified.

PLEASE ANSWER ALL QUESTIONS FULLY TAKING INTO CONSIDERATION YOUR OWN CORPORATE NEEDS.

The bidder would then be aware from the substantive tender pack that there is a requirement to confirm its own expectations for the project at each of the key stages. The bid information pack should contain the same level of information from the authority's perspective, but should include a note stating that it is not anticipated that the contract or will have the same response as that of the contracting authority, rather that it is the individual stakeholder perspective that is required. The problem that arises from this, however, is that this cannot be a scored element. Contractors often do not give much thought or time to the parts of a bid that have no scoring element. One way to overcome that is to confirm that while it is not a scored portion of a bid, it will become a contractual mechanism based on collaborative working processes. The VfM tracking mechanism will not be without flaws, but it is anticipated that, over time, these flaws will be ironed out and an effective mechanism developed.

It is then envisaged that from this initial bidding exercise, that a form of protocol be developed, a specimen of follows.

PROTOCOL

(A) This protocol is intended as a guide to help all participants undertaking a capital build infrastructure project and other projects achieve a value for money solution, which serves all parties to the contract.

(B) The aim of the protocol is that all participants work collaboratively to achieve a value for money solution; and that this protocol is not intended to become a contractual mechanism bringing about termination triggers, rather it is intended to be used throughout the project as a mechanism to assist in the achievement of VfM and or identify in the early stages of the project what issues are arising that might impact on the achievement of VfM.

(C) The protocol takes into consideration that each project is different and that unknown unknowns and project risks inevitably have an impact on the achievement of value for oney; this is one of the main reasons why the protocol is based on different targets set out at the beginning of each project.

(D) The mechanism is not intended to be a one-size-fits-all; it is expected that the mechanism be adapted to suit the needs of each party to the project contracts.

The author does not give permission to any party to reproduce, copy, disseminate or use the drafting as precedent for future documentation without express written permission, which shall be considered on merit by emailing info@avac-ltd.co.uk or Taylor & Francis Publishing.

122 *VfM protocol and other documents*

The core principles for achieving value for money and implementing the tracking

Value for money assessments currently being undertaken are significantly flawed, in that there is a lack of a mechanism to track the achievement or not of value for money as an ongoing collaborative working toolkit.

1 Working collaboratively – setting expectations and milestones early

At the commencement of every project, each party to the project will have undertaken some form of feasibility study or business plan. Within this exercise, each participant will have set out the aims and expectations to be achieved from the project. The protocol envisages that participants will be transparent in declaring their aims and expectations. The protocol also envisages that each participant will have a number of different aims and expectations, which will be achievable at different periods of time throughout the life of the project. The protocol expects that each party will have an early discourse about where the individual milestones will be achieved or become achievable.

2 Purpose of milestones and understanding value

The purpose of setting identifiable milestones at an early stage by each participant, establishes a baseline of where the parties to the project expect to achieve a value for the work, time and costs dedicated to the project up to and including that point in time. Setting the milestones also assists with a collaborative understanding of where the values of a project sit for each participant. The protocol then expects that the achievement of value for money can be achieved if all parties work together for the benefit of each other to achieve all parties' goals. But the tracking process can be measured using the agreed milestones at the agreed key stages.

3 Tracking the achievement of expectations

As the project progresses the protocol requires each of the stakeholders engaged on the project to attend identified project meetings. During each meeting, an agenda item must be set to include VfM position to date.

At each meeting, every stakeholder should attend fully prepared with visual (graphical) information showing where the prevailing VfM position is at the identified key stage and the fluctuation or trend to date. This should be supported by a report on how the trend is likely to progress towards the next scheduled meeting to identify any project risks that may lie ahead in the next stage and key phase and what the likely outcome of these are.

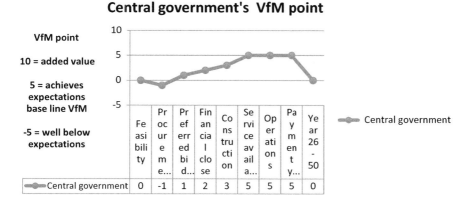

Figure 6.1 Central government

An example of the graphical information required is shown in Figure 6.1.

It is expected that the information gathered as part of this process during the project life will provide tangible and contemporaneous data not only to show that the local authority is compliant with its duty of best value, but also that each stakeholder is taking on board the importance of VfM, in a project-specific environment.

4 Identification of risk

The identification of risk should align with the schedule of risks developed within any given workshop and if there are any new risks identified these should be fed into the risk process as a separate exercise.

It is expected that the protocol forms part of the contract documents as a schedule. In terms of the form of contract then additional drafting should be included in the head agreement to ensure that the protocol is implemented by the contractor and that, in turn, the subcontractors, as stakeholders, also provide equal information.

It would also be necessary to include project specific drafting in terms of ensuring that while not providing the information would not trigger a termination on its own, if there were multiple incidences of the information not being provided, then this would be seen as minor breaches, reflecting against the achievement of key performance indicators and quality.

While it is not anticipated that breaching the requirement to provide the information should be a major non-compliance, there has to be some form of incentive within the contracts to ensure that the information is provided by all parties.

Conclusion

This book set out on a voyage of discovery to understand why so much importance was placed on the concept of VfM, not only in the UK, but also in a worldwide arena, having discovered that there is no real definition of VfM and that there is no real mechanism to test or track whether VfM is being or has been achieved on a project-specific basis. The book then sought to open up debate and provide an idea, concept or protocol that could be used in the future to measure VfM. By utilising the ETM as a tracking mechanism or, indeed, any other form of tracking mechanism, at least when there are heated debates about whether VfM has or has not been achieved, there will be contemporaneous evidence to rebut any erroneous debate.

Without such a mechanism, these debates really are futile.

Index

Aboriginals 20–21, 22, 24
accountability 14, 20, 49, 60
accounting 33, 52, 53, 65, 71
African Nationalist Congress (ANC) 31–32
Akbar 35
Apartheid 29, 31–32, 33, 44
architecture 70, 79, 82, 87–88, 97
Arrowsmith, S. 11
audit mechanisms 2–3, 13–15, 19–20, 25, 33, 39, 43, 61, 84
Aurangzeb 35
Australia 20–26; overview 20–22; early years 22–23; EU and 25–26; VfM requirements and expectations 1, 25–26, 44; World War I and aftermath 23–24; World War II and aftermath 24–25
Australian Department of Infrastructure and Regional Development 25–26
Australian National Audit Office 25

Bank of England 65
banks/financiers: aims and incentives **63–64**; roles and responsibilities 32, 59; tracking values 99, **100–109**, 110, 111, 112, 113, 117; VfM stages and 83, 87, **91–95**, 98
beneficiaries: aims and incentives **63–64**, 74; categories of 73; reputation of 85; risk and 82, 87, 98, 120; roles and responsibilities 34, 59, **63–64**, 69–70, 72–74, 73; tracking values 99, **100–109**, 110–11, *115*, *117*; VfM stages and 80–81; VfM value and fluctuations **91–95**
Beveridge Report (UK) 6–7
bidding stage: financial/contract close and 87, **103**, 113–14; procurement

process and 81–83, 87, 98, **101**, 113–14, 119–21; profit motive and 71; risk and 82, 87, 98, 120–21; tracking values 98, 99, **101**, **102**, 110, 111, 112, 113–14; VfM value and fluctuations **91**
Black Wednesday 12
Boer Wars 28–29
Botha, P.W. 32
budgetary controls 13–14, 25, 26, 33, 61, 67, 68, 111, 115–16
Building Information Modeling (BIM) 79
Byatt Report 51–53

central government: aims and incentives 62, **63–64**, 66; risk and 61, **63**, 65; roles and responsibilities 59, 60–63, 65–66; tracking values 99, **100–109**, 110, 116, *117*, *123*; VfM value and fluctuations **91–95**
Chamberlain, Neville 6
Chartered Institute of Builders (CIOB) 119
Chevaline 8
China 13–20; overview 13–15, 21, 27; early years 15–17; EU and 19–20; legislation 14, 19–20; VfM requirements and expectations 1, 13, 14–15, 19–20, 44, 51, 56; World War I and aftermath 17–18, 24; World War II and aftermath 18–19
Chin Dynasty 15
Chinese Audit Office 14, 19
Ch'ing Dynasty 17
Chola Empire 35
Chou Dynasty 15
Churchill, Winston 4
Common Market 7

126 Index

Communist Party of China 18
Companies Act 70–71
comparator tests 15, 25, 44, *45–49*, 50–51
compulsory competitive tendering (CCT) 10–11, 51
Confucianism 15–16
construction: beneficiaries and 80; contract documents and 95; contracting and 69; defects period 84–85, 87–88, **93**, 98, *114*; defined 59; economic benefit and 72; evaluation criteria 55; performance measurement framework (PMF) and 77; project timing and 61; tracking values **104**, 110, 116, 117; VfM value and fluctuations **91–95**
Construction Industry Council (CIC) 50, 75, 119
Construction Research and Innovation Strategy Panel (CRiSP) 52
consultants 59, 72
consumerism 9, 14, 44
contractors: aims and incentives **63–64**; defined 69; roles and responsibilities 59, 68–72, 85; tracking values 99, **100–109**, 110, *114*, *115*; VfM stages and 79–80, 82–83, 85, 87–88, 98; VfM value and fluctuations **91–95**; *see also* bidding; subcontractors
contracts/contract documents: analysis of 95; apportionment of risk 59; drafting 119–24; ethics and 8; post-contract years 86, 88, **94**, 99, **108–9**; VfM stages and 83
corruption: China and 14, 16, 17, 18, 19–20, 44; South Africa and 27, 33–34, 44, 49; UK and 2–3, 4, 11; UNCITRAL and 55; VfM testing and *46*, 49, 55, 120

debt funders 59, 62, 63, 68–69, 80, **100–109**, *112*–114, *117*
De Clerk, F. W. 32
defects period 84–85, 87–88, **93**, 98, 114
DeLorean project 11
Deng Xiaoping 19
deregulation 10–11, 25
design: beneficiaries and 74; contract documents and 95; defined 59; expectations and 79–81; profits and 71; risk and 70, 75, 79–80, 81; VfM stages and 79, 82, 85, 87, 98

development projects 51, 52, 73
discrimination 29, 31
Dutch East India Trading Company 27, 28

economic costs 51–52
economic development, role of 1, 5, 8, 10, 39, 43–44
Elizabeth II (queen) 22, 25
English East India Company 27
Equilibrium Testing Mechanism (ETM) i, 118, 124
equity funders 69, **100–109**, *113*, *117*
European Commission 54
European Free Trade Area 7
European Monetary Union 11
European PPP Expertise Centre (EPEC) 53
European Steel and Coal Community 7
European Trading Area 7
European Union (EU): Australia and 25–26; China and 19–20; inactivity of 9; India and 37–38; MEAT provision 54, 56; origins of 7; South Africa and 32–34; transparency and 8, 9, 10–12; UK and 9–12
Exchange Rate Mechanism (ERM) 11–12
Exchequer and Audit Act 3

facilities management (FM): defined 59; tracking 98, **106**, **107**, 114, *115*, *117*; VfM stages and 85, 88; VfM value and fluctuations **91–95**
feasibility stage 77–81, 87, **91**, 97–98, **100**, 120, 122
Federation Internationale Des Des Ingénieurs-Conseils (FIDIC) 119–20
Ferranti Case 8
fiduciary duty 59–60, 61, 65–67, 71, 83
financial close 83; delays and 69; tracking values 87, 98, **103**, 111, 112, 113, 114, 117; VfM value and fluctuations **91**
financiers *See* banks/financiers
free markets 5, 8–9, 10, 13, 34, 38, 44, 60
free trade 5, 7, 8–9
funders 59, 72, 80, 112–18; *see also* debt funders; private sector funders; public sector funders

Gladstone, William 2
Gong, T. 14

Green Book provisions 12, 53, 56, 62, 66, 71, 78
Green Revolution 37
Gregory, M. 77

handover period 84–85, 87–88, **93**, 98
Han Dynasty 15–16
Her Majesty's Treasury (HMT) 53, 56, 65, 67, 68, 78, 84
Hodge 53

India 34–38; overview 34; early years 35–36; EU and 37–38; legislation 49; VfM requirements and expectations 1, 38, 44, 49, 56; World War I and aftermath 36; World War II and aftermath 36–37
Indian National Congress 35–36
inflation 11, 18
Infrastructure Australia 25–26
Infrastructure UK 14–15
insurance industry 75
International Federation of Consulting Engineers (FIDIC) 119–20
International Monetary Fund (IMF) 32, 37
International Project Finance Association 69

Joint Contracts Tribunal (JCT) 95, 119–20

Korean War 7
Kushna Empire 35

Latham Report 53, 60
legal development, role of 1, 12, 43–44, 55–56
lifecycle period 85–86, 88, **94**, 98
Liu, J. 77
local government: aims and incentives **63–64**, 66, 73; roles and responsibilities 59, 66–68; tracking values 99, **100–109**, 110, *116*; VfM value and fluctuations **91–95**
Local Government Act 9, 11, 66, 85

Maastricht Treaty 11
maintenance period 85–86, 88, **91–95**, 98, **106**, **108–9**
Major, John 51
Mandela, Nelson 32
Mao Zedong 18–19

marketing 70, 80, 82
market value 52
Menzies, Robert 24
milestones 52, 83, 86–88, 89, 97–99, 110, 111, 122
Ming Dynasty 17
Mongols 17
Most Economically Advantageous Tender (MEAT) 54, 56
Mughal Empire 35

nationalisation 4, 5, 7, 9–10, 13, 16, 27–28, 37, 52
nationalism 18, 30
Nationalist Party of China 18
NEC contract 95
Neely, A. 77
Nehru, Jawaharlal 37
New Engineering Contract (NEC) 119–20

operations management *see* facilities management (FM)
opinion polls 70, 80, 82
Opium Wars 17
options appraisals 53, 62, 66
Organisation for Economic Cooperation and Development (OECD) 50

Pan Africanist Congress (PAC) 31–32
PAYE system 7
Performance Measurement Framework (PMF) 77
Performance Prism 77
Platts, K. 77
political development, role of 1, 39, 43–44, 55–56
post-contract years 86, 88, **94**, 99, **108–9**
price fixing 13
Private Finance Initiative (PFI) 12, 45, 50, 51, 53
Private Sector Comparator (PSC) 15, 25, 45–48, 50–51
private sector contractors *see* contractors; professional advisors; subcontractors
private sector funders **63–64**, 68–72
privatisation 10–11, 12, 51
procurement stage 81–83; for PPP collaboration 12, 15, 33, 38, 39; risk and 82, 87, 98, 120–21; timeline of VfM tests 45–48; tracking values 99, **101**, 110, 111; UNCITRAL and 14, 33, 38, 44, 48, 49, 54–56, 61; VfM

128 *Index*

value and fluctuations **90**; WTO rules and 19
professional advisors 69–70
profit, as incentive 71
"Prudential Code" 65
Public Accounts Committee (PAC) 1, 2–3, 5–6, 8, 9, 11, 43–44
Public Contracts Regulations (PCR) 54, 55, 56, 61
public-private partnerships (PPP) 12, 15, 33, 38, 39, 44, *45*
"Public Sector Business Cases using the Five Case Model" (HMT) 78–81
public sector comparator tests 25, 44, *45*–49, 51
public sector contractors *see* contractors; professional advisors; subcontractors
public sector funders 62, 63, 65, 68, 78, 81–82
public spending 1, 2, 3, 5, 6–7, 8, 11–12
Public Works Loan Board (PWLB) 65
purchasers 8–9, 61–62, 66–68, 79, 81, 85

racism 29, 31; *see also* Apartheid
Rand Revolt 30
risk: apportionment of 59; benchmarking and 57; beneficiaries and 82, 87, 98, 120; bidding and 82, 87, 98, 120–21; central government and 61, **63**, 65; collective 59; debt funders and 69; design expectations and 70, 75, 79–80, 81; feasibility and 78; fluctuation of 57–58, 81, 84, 89, 119, 122; Green Book provisions and 53, 71; identification of 89, **91**–**95**, 95, 110, 123; lifecycle and maintenance stage 88, 98; passing of 43; post-contract 88; private sector and 70, 71; procurement and 82, 87, 98, 120–21; reward and 74–76; risk of finance and 50–51; tracking values 99, **101**–**5**, 110, 118; works stage and 84, 87, 98
risk transfer 33
Roy 71
Royal Institute of British Architects (RIBA) 87, 97–99
Royal Institute of Chartered Surveyors (RICS) 119
Rutherford, B. 43, 70
Ryrie Rules 50–51

sector-specific groups *see* stakeholders
segregation 31
senior debt funders *112, 113*

service availability **92**, **105**, 114, 116, 117
service users **63**–**64**, 69–70, 73
Shang Dynasty 15
Single European Act 8
slavery 27
SLEEPT 43
Smuts, Jan 31
social class 5, 6, 23–24, 38
socioeconomic development, role of 1, 6–7, 12, 39, 43–44, 55–56
Song Dynasty 16–17
South Africa 26–34; overview 26–28; early years 28–29; EU and 32–34; legislation 29–30, 31, 33, 44; VfM requirements and expectations 1, 27, 34, 44, 49; World War I and aftermath 29–31; World War II and aftermath 31–32
stakeholders 59–76; aims and incentives 52–53, 56, 57–58, 60, **63**–**64**, 74, 75; defined 59–60; fiduciary duty and 59–60, 61, 65–67, 71, 83; liability and reputation of 84–85; tracking values 52–53, 57–58, 86–95, 97–99, **100**–**109**, 110–18, *123*; VfM value and fluctuations **91**–**95**; *see also specific stakeholder*
subcontractors 59, 69–70, 79, 123
Sui Dynasty 16
surveys, customer 70, 80, 82

T'ang Dynasty 16
Tata Steel Mills 36
taxation: in Australia 23, 24; beneficiaries and 73, 74; in China 16, 17, 18; in India 35; in South Africa 34; in UK 7, 12, 66
tendering requirements: bidding and 121; in China 44; compulsory competitive tendering (CCT) 10–11, 51; MEAT provisions and 54, 56; timelines for 46, 48; tracking values and 99, **101**, 110; in UK 9, 10–12, 44, 51; UNCITRAL and 55–56
testing/tracking mechanisms 43–58; aims and objectives 2–3, 57–58, 65–66, 86–96, 99–109, 124; comparator tests 15, 25, 44, *45*–49, 50–51; as contractual requirement 118, 119–24; development of 11–12, 43–44, 72, 75, 77, 81, 86, 89–95, 97–118; Equilibrium Testing Mechanism (ETM) i, 118, 124; how to 86–88, 97–99; look-back tests 66; one-size-fits-all testing 72; origins of 1, 12;

RIBA plan and 87–88, 97–99; software 50; timeline of VfM tests 44, *45–48*; tracking values 52–53, 57–58, 86–95, 97–99, **100–109**, 110–18, *123*; visualisation of **91–95**, 95, 110–18, 122–23; *see also specific stage*

Thatcher government 10–11

trade deficits 8, 46

trade liberalisation 10

trade unions 4, 9–10

transparency: audits and 13–14; central government and 60–61; China and 19–20; cost controls and 28; EU and 8, 9, 10–12; India and 49; public value tests and 26, *45–48*; trade and 9; UK and 53; UNCITRAL Model Law and 14, 33, 38, 44, 54–56; VfM "overlap" and 11

transparency of dealings 11, 28, 44–45, 120

UK Department for Business Innovation and Skills 52

UK East India Company 36

UK National Audit Office 61

UK National Infrastructure Plan (2014) 52

UNCITRAL Model Law 14, 33, 38, 44, 48, 49, 54–56, 61

United Kingdom (UK) 1–12; overview 1, 13, 14–15, 21–22, 27; early years 2–3, 15, 28–29, 35–36; EU and 9–12; legislation 2–3, 8, 9, 10–12, 50–52, 53, 54; VfM requirements and expectations 1–2, 3, 6, 9, 11, 12, 14–15, 38, 43–44, 50–53, 85; World War I and aftermath 3–6, 23–24, 29, 36; World War II and aftermath 6–9, 20, 24–26, 31, 32–33, 36–37

United Nations 20

United States 4, 6, 7, 8, 17, 18, 20, 24

VfM (Value for Money) 43–58, 77–96; concept of 9, 11, 12, 27, 43–44, 50; core principles 122–24; definitions 3, 11, 49–57, 124; early references to 6, 25; fluctuation of 43, 57–58, 72, 76, 81, 83, 88–95, **91–95**, 99, 119, 122; growth in use of 50; legislative parameters 50; non-commercialised activities and 52–53; overview of stages 77–86; SLEEPT and 43; subjectivity of 1, 43, 54; *see also* testing/tracking mechanisms; *specific stage or phase*

Wanna, J. 25

White Australia Party 22, 24

works stage 83, 84, 85, 87–88, **90**, 98, **104**

World Bank 20, 37

World Trade Organisation (WTO) 19–20

World War I 3–6, 17–18, 23–24, 29–31, 36

World War II 6–9, 18–19, 20, 24–26, 31–33, 36–37